EDITOR: Maryanne Blacker

FOOD EDITOR: Pamela Clark

DESIGN DIRECTOR: Neil Carlyle

• • •

DESIGNER: Louise McGeachie

• • •

DEPUTY FOOD EDITOR: Jan Castorina

ASSISTANT FOOD EDITORS: Karen Green, Kathy Snowball

ASSOCIATE FOOD EDITORS: Karen Lau, Enid Morrison

CHIEF HOME ECONOMIST: Kathy Wharton

DEPUTY CHIEF HOME ECONOMIST: Louise Patniotis

HOME ECONOMISTS: Sheena Chisholm, Tracey Kern, Quinton Kohler, Jill Lange, Voula Mantzouridis, Alexandra McCowan, Kathy McGarry, Dimitra Stais

EDITORIAL COORDINATOR: Elizabeth Hooper

KITCHEN ASSISTANT: Amy Wong

• • •

FOOD STYLISTS: Marie-Helene Clauzon, Rosemary de Santis, Carolyn Fienberg, Michelle Gorry, Jacqui Hing

PHOTOGRAPHERS: Kevin Brown, Robert Clark, Robert Taylor, Jon Waddy

• • •

HOME LIBRARY STAFF:

ASSISTANT EDITOR: Judy Newman

DESIGNER: Robbylee Phelan

SECRETARY: Sanchia Roth

• • •

PUBLISHER: Richard Walsh

DEPUTY PUBLISHER: Graham Lawrence

ASSISTANT PUBLISHER: Bob Neil

Produced by The Australian Women's Weekly Home Library. Typeset by Photoset Computer Service Pty Ltd, and Letter Perfect, Sydney. Printed by Dai Nippon Co., Ltd in Japan. Published by Australian Consolidated Press, 54 Park Street Sydney. Distributed by Network Distribution Company, 54 Park Street Sydney. Distributed in New Zealand by Netlink Distribution Company (9) 302 7616. Distributed in the U.K. by Australian Consolidated Press (UK) Ltd, (0604) 760 456. Distributed in Canada by Whitecap Books Ltd, (604) 9809852. Distributed in South Africa by Intermag (011) 4933200.

Mediterranean Cookbook

Includes index.
ISBN 0 949128 45 7.

1. Cookery. 2. Mediterranean. (Series: Australian Women's Weekly Home Library).

641.591822

• • •

• • •

COVER: Clockwise from left on back cover: Chick Peas with Pepperoni and Bacon (page 91), Octopus and Red Wine Stew (page 50), Seafood Paella (page 53), Rigatoni with Broccoli and Sun-Dried Tomatoes (page 81), Sauteed Pepper and Salami Salad (page 97), Olive and Herb Bread (page 89), Roast Lamb (page 76) served with Spicy Potato Bake (page 90), Vine Leaf and Beef Rolls (page 18) and Grilled Snapper in Honey Fennel Marinade (page 57).
Basket, chair, jars (right) and mortar (centre) from Appley Hoare Antiques; terracotta tiles from Pazotti; marble tiles from Country Floors; serving ware from Corso de Fiori, Accoutrement and Villa Italiana; fabric from Les Olivades

MEDITERRANEAN COOKBOOK

From the many colourful cuisines around the Mediterranean area came the inspiration for the recipes in this book. Here, you'll find many ingredients that are favourites of people in the region, such as fresh vegetables, eggplants, tomatoes, olives, spices and fresh herbs, all mixed and matched in a mouth-watering variety of dishes. Scrumptious desserts, cakes and pastries are wonderful, too. We've made no attempt to be truly authentic, but have recreated the style of food you'd be eating if you travelled there. Some ingredients may be unfamiliar but are explained in the glossary on page 124.

Pamela Clark

FOOD EDITOR

2	SOUPS	70	LAMB
12	ENTREES	78	VEGETARIAN
32	POULTRY AND RABBIT	84	ACCOMPANIMENTS
42	SEAFOOD	98	CAKES AND DESSERTS
58	BEEF	124	GLOSSARY
64	PORK AND VEAL	126	INDEX

BRITISH & NORTH AMERICAN READERS: Please note that conversion charts for cup and spoon measurements and oven temperatures are on page 128.

SOUPS

Wonderful meals are made of soups like these. Most are robust and substantial, based on peasant-style cooking where people put what they had (vegetables, beans, peas and lentils, pasta or grains) into the pot, and, with long slow cooking, lovingly transformed them into meals to remember. Meat, chicken and fish, often scarce, would be added when possible, but there was little pattern; the soups were usually different from day to day. Other soups in this section are along famous traditional lines, such as egg and lemon soup, and chilled, refreshing gazpacho. All can be served with fresh, crusty bread for extra enjoyment.

TROUT AND CELERY SOUP

40g butter
2 green shallots, chopped
3 sticks celery, sliced
½ teaspoon ground cumin
½ teaspoon ground coriander
½ teaspoon ground ginger
pinch chilli powder
pinch turmeric
¼ cup plain flour
150g ocean trout fillet
¼ bunch (10 leaves) English spinach, shredded
¼ cup cream

FISH STOCK
500g fish bones
1½ litres (6 cups) water
½ cup dry white wine
1 small onion, chopped
1 stick celery, chopped
½ teaspoon fennel seeds, crushed
2 bay leaves
8 black peppercorns

Heat butter in pan, add shallots, celery, cumin, coriander, ginger, chilli and turmeric, cook, stirring, until celery is just tender. Stir in flour, stir over heat 1 minute. Remove from heat, gradually stir in 1 litre (4 cups) of the fish stock. Stir over heat until mixture boils and thickens.

Remove skin from trout, cut flesh into 1cm pieces. Add trout, spinach and cream to soup, stir over heat until trout is tender.
Fish Stock: Combine washed bones, water, wine, onion, celery, fennel seeds, bay leaves and peppercorns in pan. Bring to boil, simmer, uncovered, 20 minutes. Strain stock, discard bones and mixture. Freeze any remaining cold stock.

Serves 6.

■ Soup can be made 2 days ahead.
■ Storage: Covered, in refrigerator.
■ Freeze: Suitable.
■ Microwave: Suitable.

LENTIL SOUP WITH CORIANDER AND TOMATOES

1 tablespoon olive oil
2 onions, chopped
2 cloves garlic, crushed
¾ cup red lentils
2 x 410g cans tomatoes
2 litres (8 cups) water
2 small chicken stock cubes, crumbled
⅓ cup chopped fresh parsley
⅓ cup chopped fresh coriander
2 teaspoons turmeric
1 teaspoon paprika
1 teaspoon cracked black peppercorns
pinch ground cumin

Heat oil in pan, add onions and garlic, cook, stirring, until onions are soft. Stir in lentils, undrained crushed tomatoes, water, stock cubes, parsley, coriander, turmeric, paprika and peppercorns, bring to boil, simmer, uncovered, about 1½ hours or until lentils are tender.

Reserve 2 cups of soup; blend or process remaining soup in batches until smooth. Combine pureed soup and reserved soup in pan, stir until heated through. Sprinkle soup with cumin just before serving.

Serves 6.

■ Soup can be made 3 days ahead.
■ Storage: Covered, in refrigerator.
■ Freeze: Suitable.
■ Microwave: Suitable.

RIGHT: From left: Lentil Soup with Coriander and Tomatoes, Trout and Celery Soup.

Combine chicken, water, onion, carrot, peppercorns and bay leaf in pan. Bring to boil, simmer, partially covered, 30 minutes. Remove chicken, strain stock into bowl, discard vegetable mixture. Return chicken to stock, cool, cover, refrigerate several hours or overnight.

Quarter peppers, remove seeds and membranes. Grill peppers, skin side up, until skin blisters and blackens. Peel skin, cut peppers into thin strips.

Skim fat from stock, remove chicken from stock, remove skin and meat from bones, discard skin and bones; cut meat into fine slices.

Heat stock in pan, add peppers and stock cube, bring to boil, simmer, uncovered, 10 minutes.

Just before serving, stir in herbs, sugar and peppercorns. Remove and discard bay leaf.

Serves 6.

■ Soup can be prepared a day ahead.
■ Storage: Covered, in refrigerator.
■ Freeze: Stock suitable.
■ Microwave: Suitable.

LAMB AND CHICK PEA SOUP

1 cup (200g) chick peas
3 lamb leg chops
2 tablespoons olive oil
2 onions, chopped
2 x 410g cans tomatoes
3 litres (12 cups) water
2 small beef stock cubes, crumbled
1 bay leaf
¼ teaspoon ground saffron
½ teaspoon ground ginger
50g vermicelli pasta
½ cup chopped fresh parsley

Place peas in large bowl, cover with water, stand overnight.

Rinse peas, drain well. Cut lamb into 1cm cubes; discard bones. Heat oil in pan, add lamb, stir over heat until well browned. Add onions, cook, stirring, until onions are soft. Stir in peas, undrained crushed tomatoes, water, stock cubes, bay leaf, saffron and ginger, bring to boil, simmer, uncovered, about 2 hours or until peas are tender. Add vermicelli, simmer, uncovered, until pasta is just tender.

Just before serving, remove and discard bay leaf, stir in parsley.

Serves 6.

■ Soup can be made 3 days ahead.
■ Storage: Covered, in refrigerator.
■ Freeze: Suitable.
■ Microwave: Suitable.

VEGETABLE SOUP WITH PISTOU

1 medium leek, chopped
2 carrots, chopped
1 potato, chopped
1 onion, chopped
1 zucchini, chopped
1 tomato, chopped
2 litres (8 cups) water
½ cup small macaroni
200g frozen broad beans
200g frozen peas
310g can canellini beans, rinsed, drained

PISTOU
½ cup grated fresh parmesan cheese
½ cup chopped fresh basil
3 cloves garlic, crushed
½ cup olive oil

Combine leek, carrots, potato, onion, zucchini, tomato and water in large pan. Bring to boil, simmer, covered, about 45 minutes or until vegetables are tender.

Add macaroni, broad beans and peas, simmer, covered, 15 minutes.

Add canellini beans, simmer, uncovered, about 5 minutes or until heated through.

Just before serving, drop spoonfuls of pistou into soup.

Pistou: Blend or process all ingredients until smooth.

Serves 8.

■ Soup can be made a day ahead.
■ Storage: Covered, in refrigerator.
■ Freeze: Not suitable.
■ Microwave: Not suitable.

RED PEPPER SOUP

2 chicken thigh cutlets
3 litres (12 cups) water
1 onion, chopped
1 carrot, chopped
4 black peppercorns
1 bay leaf
4 red peppers
1 small chicken stock cube, crumbled
1 tablespoon chopped fresh mint
1 tablespoon chopped fresh marjoram
2 teaspoons sugar
1 teaspoon cracked black peppercorns

ABOVE: Vegetable Soup with Pistou.
RIGHT: From top: Lamb and Chick Pea Soup, Red Pepper Soup.

Above: Plate and bowl from Corso de Fiori.
Right: Shell dish from Sandy de Beyer

SEAFOOD TOMATO SOUP WITH GARLIC MAYONNAISE TOAST

300g snapper fillets
18 (about 750g) mussels
1 onion, sliced
1 tablespoon lemon juice
15 black peppercorns
1 bay leaf
2 vegetable stock cubes, crumbled
3 litres (12 cups) water
pinch turmeric
2 tablespoons olive oil
1 onion, finely chopped, extra
3 cloves garlic, crushed
1kg tomatoes, seeded
½ cup tomato paste
1 tablespoon sugar
5 saffron strands
¼ teaspoon ground fennel
1 bunch (40 leaves) English spinach, finely shredded
1 small French bread stick

GARLIC MAYONNAISE
2 egg yolks
4 cloves garlic, crushed
⅔ cup olive oil
2 teaspoons tomato paste
pinch chilli powder
1 tablespoon chopped fresh chives

Remove skin from fish, discard skin; remove any bones from fish; reserve bones. Cut fish into small cubes; scrub mussels, remove beards.

Combine bones, sliced onion, juice, peppercorns, bay leaf, stock cubes, water and turmeric in large pan, bring to boil, simmer, uncovered, 20 minutes; skim stock occasionally during cooking.

Strain stock into bowl; discard mixture. Return stock to pan, bring to boil, simmer, uncovered, about 10 minutes or until liquid is reduced by half.

Heat oil in pan, add extra onion and garlic, cook, stirring, until onion is soft. Add chopped tomatoes, paste, sugar, saffron and fennel, cook, stirring, over heat about 10 minutes or until tomatoes are soft.

Add tomato mixture to stock, bring to boil, simmer, uncovered, about 40 minutes or until soup is slightly thickened.
Just before serving, add seafood and spinach to soup, simmer, covered, until seafood is tender. Serve soup with toasted French bread stick slices, spread with garlic mayonnaise.
Garlic Mayonnaise: Blend egg yolks and garlic until pale in colour. While motor is operating, gradually add oil in a thin stream. Add tomato paste and chilli powder, blend until combined. Transfer mixture to bowl, stir in chives.

Serves 6.
■ Soup can be prepared a day ahead. Mayonnaise can be made 3 days ahead.
■ Storage: Both, covered, in refrigerator.
■ Freeze: Not suitable.
■ Microwave: Not suitable.

BROAD BEAN SOUP WITH OMELETTE CHUNKS

20g butter
1 clove garlic, crushed
2 onions, chopped
2 bacon rashers, chopped
500g fresh or frozen broad beans
1 large potato, chopped
2 sticks celery, chopped
1 litre (4 cups) water
2 large chicken stock cubes, crumbled

OMELETTE CHUNKS
2 bacon rashers, chopped
100g ham, chopped
3 eggs, lightly beaten
½ cup packaged breadcrumbs
2 tablespoons chopped fresh parsley
20g butter

Heat butter in pan, add garlic, onions and bacon, cook, stirring, until onions are soft. Add beans, potato and celery, cook, stirring, 1 minute. Add water and stock cubes, bring to boil, simmer, covered, about 1 hour or until vegetables are tender. Blend or process one-third of the soup until smooth, return to remaining soup in pan, stir over heat until boiling.
Just before serving, spoon soup into serving bowls, top with omelette chunks.
Omelette Chunks: Combine bacon, ham, eggs, breadcrumbs and parsley in bowl; mix well, stand mixture 1 hour at room temperature.

Heat butter in pan, press omelette mixture into pan, cook over low heat until firm; cool, cut into squares.

Serves 6.
■ Soup can be prepared a day ahead.
■ Storage: Covered, in refrigerator.
■ Freeze: Not suitable.
■ Microwave: Soup suitable.

MEATBALL AND PASTA SOUP

2½ litres (10 cups) water
3 small beef stock cubes, crumbled
1 onion, chopped
1 clove garlic, crushed
150g tagliatelle pasta
2 tablespoons chopped fresh basil
¼ cup chopped fresh parsley

MEATBALLS
500g minced beef
2 green shallots, finely chopped
¼ cup grated fresh parmesan cheese
¼ cup stale breadcrumbs
2 tablespoons chopped fresh parsley
1 egg, lightly beaten

Combine water, stock cubes, onion and garlic in large pan, bring to boil, simmer, uncovered, 15 minutes. Add pasta, simmer, uncovered, further 10 minutes. Add herbs and meatballs , simmer, uncovered, about 5 minutes or until meatballs are heated through.
Meatballs: Combine beef, shallots, parmesan, breadcrumbs, parsley and egg in bowl; mix well. Roll level teaspoons of mixture into balls. Place balls in shallow baking dish, bake, uncovered, in moderate oven for about 20 minutes or until browned and cooked through.

Serves 6.
■ Recipe can be prepared a day ahead.
■ Storage: Covered, in refrigerator.
■ Microwave: Suitable.
■ Freeze: Meatballs suitable.

LEFT: Clockwise from top left: Broad Bean Soup with Omelette Chunks, Meatball and Pasta Soup, Seafood Tomato Soup with Garlic Mayonnaise Toast.

Bowls from Corso de Fiori; tiles from Pazotti

GAZPACHO

1 green pepper
6 large (about 1½kg) ripe tomatoes, peeled
1 small green cucumber, peeled
1 onion, chopped
1 clove garlic, crushed
1 cup tomato juice
2 tablespoons olive oil
½ teaspoon sugar
2 tablespoons chopped fresh parsley
2 tablespoons flaked almonds, toasted

Quarter pepper, remove seeds and membrane. Grill pepper, skin side up, until skin blisters and blackens. Peel skin, chop pepper roughly. Remove and discard seeds from tomatoes and cucumber, chop vegetables roughly.

Blend or process pepper, tomatoes, cucumber, onion, garlic, juice, oil and sugar in batches until smooth. Pour into bowl, refrigerate.

Just before serving, sprinkle gazpacho with parsley and almonds.
Serves 4.
■ Gazpacho can be made a day ahead.
■ Storage: Covered, in refrigerator.
■ Freeze: Not suitable.
■ Microwave: Not suitable.

CHICK PEA SOUP WITH HERBED CREPES

1¼ cups (250g) chick peas
¼ cup olive oil
10 (about 100g) slices prosciutto, sliced
1 onion, finely chopped
2 cloves garlic, crushed
1 medium leek, sliced
1 teaspoon curry powder
1 tomato, chopped
3 litres (12 cups) water
1 large chicken stock cube, crumbled
pinch chilli powder

HERBED CREPES
⅓ cup plain flour
⅓ cup milk
1 egg, lightly beaten
1 tablespoon chopped fresh basil
1 tablespoon chopped fresh chives
1 tablespoon chopped fresh coriander

Place peas in large bowl, cover with water, stand overnight. Rinse peas, drain, place in pan, cover with water, simmer, covered, about 1 hour or until tender; drain.

Heat oil in large pan, add prosciutto, cook, stirring until crisp, drain on absorbent paper. Add onion, garlic and leek to pan, cook, stirring, until onion is soft, add curry powder and tomato, cook mixture further 5 minutes or until tomato is soft.

Add peas, the 12 cups water, stock cube and chilli to pan, bring to boil, simmer, uncovered, 40 minutes. Blend or process soup in batches until smooth.
Just before serving, add prosciutto and herbed crepe slices to soup.

Herbed Crepes: Sift flour into bowl, gradually stir in combined milk, egg and herbs, beat until smooth. Pour 2 to 3 tablespoons of batter into heated greased heavy-based crepe pan; cook until lightly browned underneath. Turn crepe, brown other side. Repeat with remaining batter. Tightly roll crepes, cut into 1½cm slices.

Serves 6.

- Soup can be prepared a day ahead. Prosciutto and crepes best prepared just before serving
- Storage: Soup, covered, in refrigerator.
- Freeze: Suitable.
- Microwave: Not suitable.

LEFT: Gazpacho.
ABOVE: From left: Lamb Shank and Tomato Soup, Chick Pea Soup with Herbed Crepes.

Left: Fish serviette ring from Sandy de Beyer.
Above: Serving ware from Corso de Fiori; tiles from Pazotti

LAMB SHANK AND TOMATO SOUP

1 tablespoon olive oil
3 lamb shanks
1 onion, chopped
1 leek, chopped
1 stick celery, chopped
3 bay leaves
2 litres (8 cups) water
1 teaspoon black peppercorns
3 cloves
2 tablespoons chopped fresh parsley
2 tablespoons tomato paste
410g can tomatoes
1 teaspoon dried thyme leaves
2 cloves garlic, crushed
2 tablespoons chopped fresh parsley, extra

MEATBALLS
500g minced lamb
3 cloves garlic, crushed
pinch cayenne pepper
1 egg, lightly beaten
1 cup stale breadcrumbs
2 tablespoons chopped fresh parsley
plain flour
oil for deep-frying

Heat oil in large pan, add lamb shanks, cook until well browned all over. Add onion, leek, celery, bay leaves, water, peppercorns, cloves and parsley, bring to boil, simmer, covered, 1 hour.

Strain stock into bowl, discard lamb shanks and vegetables. Cool stock, cover, refrigerate several hours or overnight.

Skim fat from stock; bring stock to boil in large pan, add paste, undrained crushed tomatoes and thyme, simmer, uncovered, 15 minutes. Add meatballs, simmer, uncovered, about 10 minutes or until meatballs are heated through.

Just before serving, add garlic and extra parsley to soup.

Meatballs: Process lamb, garlic, pepper, egg, breadcrumbs and parsley until well combined. Using floured hands, roll 2 level teaspoons of lamb mixture into a ball; repeat with remaining mixture, refrigerate 1 hour. Deep-fry meatballs in batches in hot oil until browned and cooked through; drain on absorbent paper.

Serves 6.

- Soup can be prepared a day ahead.
- Storage: Covered, in refrigerator.
- Freeze: Stock suitable.
- Microwave: Not suitable.

BEAN AND TOMATO SOUP WITH GARLIC TOASTS

¾ cup borlotti beans
¾ cup blackeye beans
3 bacon rashers, chopped
2 teaspoons olive oil
2 large onions, chopped
2 sticks celery, chopped
1 carrot, chopped
410g can tomatoes
2 tablespoons tomato paste
½ teaspoon sugar
2 small chicken stock cubes,
   crumbled
1½ litres (6 cups) water
2 tablespoons chopped fresh parsley

GARLIC TOASTS
8 slices Vienna bread
¼ cup olive oil
2 cloves garlic, crushed
2 tablespoons fresh oregano leaves
1 teaspoon fine sea salt

Place beans in bowl, cover with water, stand overnight; drain.

Add bacon to pan, cook, stirring, until bacon is lightly browned; drain on absorbent paper, reserve bacon.

Heat oil in pan, add onions, celery and carrot, cook, stirring occasionally, until carrot is tender. Add beans, undrained crushed tomatoes, paste, sugar, stock cubes and water, bring to boil, simmer, covered, about 50 minutes or until beans are tender.

Just before serving, add reserved bacon and parsley to soup, stir until heated through. Place a garlic toast in each serving bowl, pour soup over toast, serve soup with remaining garlic toasts.

Garlic Toasts: Brush both sides of bread slices with combined oil and garlic, bake in moderate oven 10 minutes; turn over, sprinkle with oregano leaves and salt, bake further 10 minutes or until lightly browned.

Serves 4.

■ Soup can be prepared a day ahead. Toasts can be made 3 hours ahead.
■ Storage: Soup, covered, in refrigerator. Cooled toasts in airtight container.
■ Freeze: Soup suitable.
■ Microwave: Soup suitable.

PEPPERED TOMATO SOUP

1 tablespoon olive oil
1 clove garlic, crushed
2 onions, chopped
8 large (about 2kg) ripe tomatoes,
   peeled, chopped
1 small chicken stock cube, crumbled
1 tablespoon tomato paste
2 teaspoons sugar
1 bay leaf
2 sprigs fresh thyme
1 teaspoon chopped fresh mint
1 teaspoon chopped fresh basil
3 cloves
pinch cayenne pepper
1 tablespoon chopped fresh
   thyme, extra
1 tablespoon chopped fresh
   basil, extra

Heat oil in pan, add garlic and onions, cook, stirring, until onions are soft. Add tomatoes, stock cube, paste, sugar, bay leaf, thyme sprigs, mint, basil, cloves and pepper, simmer, uncovered, about 20 minutes or until tomatoes have softened

and liquid is reduced by one third. Remove and discard bay leaf, thyme sprigs and cloves, blend or process soup until smooth.

Just before serving, return soup to pan, reheat, serve sprinkled with extra herbs.

Serves 4.

- Soup can be made a day ahead.
- Storage: Covered, in refrigerator.
- Freeze: Suitable.
- Microwave: Suitable.

POTATO SPINACH SOUP

20g butter
1 medium leek, sliced
2 large (about 400g) potatoes
2 litres (8 cups) water
1 large chicken stock cube, crumbled
200g ham, chopped
½ bunch (20 leaves) English spinach, shredded

Heat butter in pan, add leek, cook, stirring, until leek is soft. Cut potatoes into 1cm cubes, add to pan with water and stock cube, bring to boil, simmer, uncovered, about 20 minutes or until potatoes are soft. Add ham and spinach, stir until heated through.

Serves 6.

- Soup can be prepared a day ahead.
- Storage: Covered, in refrigerator.
- Freeze: Not suitable.
- Microwave: Suitable.

EGG AND LEMON SOUP

1.6kg boiling chicken
¼ cup lemon juice
2 litres (8 cups) water
½ cup short grain rice
2 eggs
1 egg yolk
⅓ cup lemon juice, extra

Combine chicken, juice and water in large pan, bring to boil, simmer, covered, 3 hours; cool. Transfer chicken and stock to large bowl, cover, refrigerate several hours or overnight.

Skim fat from stock, remove chicken, reserve chicken for another use; strain stock. Combine 1½ litres (6 cups) stock and rice in large pan, bring to boil, simmer, uncovered, about 12 minutes or until rice is tender. Freeze any remaining stock.

Just before serving, beat eggs and yolk in small bowl with electric mixer, gradually add extra juice and 1 cup of hot soup. Gradually add egg mixture to remaining soup in pan, cook, stirring, without boiling, until mixture is heated through.

Serves 4.

- Stock with rice can be prepared a day ahead.
- Storage: Covered, in refrigerator.
- Freeze: Not suitable.
- Microwave: Not suitable.

LEFT: Bean and Tomato Soup with Garlic Toasts.
ABOVE: Clockwise from top left: Egg and Lemon Soup, Peppered Tomato Soup, Potato Spinach Soup.

Above: Serving ware from Corso de Fiori

ENTREES & APPETISERS

Piquantly flavoured and tantalising, our recipes offer you a terrific choice of entrees and appetisers ranging from the rustic to those that are as smart as any occasion you want to plan. There are splendid fresh vegetables, and heaps of herbs, olives and garlic. Our seafood is superb, our pastries are of a mouth-watering variety. Then it will be your pleasure to discover many other treats: goats' cheese wrapped in tapenade, several tasty dips, elegant terrines and favourites such as garlic prawns and mini pizzas with prawns and artichokes.

MINCED LAMB IN VINE LEAVES

16 packaged vine leaves, rinsed, drained
125g black olives, chopped
500g minced lamb
1 small onion, finely chopped
250g packet frozen spinach, thawed, drained
2 cloves garlic, crushed
2 tablespoons chopped fresh parsley
2 teaspoons lemon juice
2 tablespoons olive oil

Lightly grease 8 ovenproof dishes (½ cup capacity).

Line each dish with vine leaves, shiny side down; allow edges to overhang dishes. Divide olives between dishes. Combine mince, onion, spinach, garlic, parsley, juice and oil in bowl; mix well.

Divide mixture evenly between dishes, press firmly, fold overhanging leaves over mince mixture, cover dishes with foil. Place dishes in baking dish with enough boiling water to come halfway up sides of ovenproof dishes. Bake in moderately hot oven 30 minutes. Remove dishes from water; cool.

Just before serving, drain dishes, turn onto serving plates.

Serves 8.

■ Recipe can be made a day ahead.
■ Storage: Covered, in refrigerator.
■ Freeze: Not suitable.
■ Microwave: Not suitable.

DEEP-FRIED CHEESE AND ANCHOVY TRIANGLES

4 slices bread
45g can anchovy fillets, rinsed, drained
75g bocconcini cheese, sliced
½ cup milk, approximately
plain flour
1 egg, lightly beaten
oil for deep-frying

TOMATO BASIL SAUCE
1 tablespoon olive oil
1 onion, sliced
1 clove garlic, crushed
410g can tomatoes
1 tablespoon tomato paste
⅓ cup water
½ small chicken stock cube, crumbled
1 tablespoon shredded fresh basil
¼ teaspoon sugar

Remove crusts from bread, spread mashed anchovies evenly over 2 slices of the bread. Top with cheese, then remaining bread. Cut each sandwich into 4 squares, dip squares into milk, then flour, then egg.

Just before serving, deep-fry squares in hot oil until browned all over; drain on absorbent paper. Cut squares in half diagonally, serve with tomato basil sauce.

Tomato Basil Sauce: Heat oil in pan, add onion and garlic, cook, stirring, until onion is soft. Stir in undrained crushed tomatoes, paste, water and stock cube. Bring to boil, simmer, uncovered, about 10 minutes or until slightly thickened, add basil and sugar, stir until heated through.

Serves 4.

■ Triangles and sauce can be prepared a day ahead.
■ Storage: Covered, in refrigerator.
■ Freeze: Not suitable.
■ Microwave: Not suitable.

MUSSELS IN HERB AND CAPER MARINADE

40 (about 600g) small mussels
2 cups water
½ cup olive oil
¼ cup red wine vinegar
2 teaspoons drained capers
1 small onion, chopped
2 cloves garlic, crushed
1 tablespoon chopped fresh parsley
1 tablespoon chopped fresh chives
½ teaspoon cracked black peppercorns

Scrub mussels; remove beards. Heat water in large pan, add mussels, cook, covered, over high heat about 3 minutes or until mussels open. Drain, discard liquid. Loosen mussels, discard half of each shell. Combine mussels with remaining ingredients in bowl, cover, refrigerate several hours or overnight.

Just before serving, return mussels to remaining shells, drizzle with marinade.

Serves 4.

■ Mussels can be prepared a day ahead.
■ Storage: Covered, in refrigerator.
■ Freeze: Not suitable.
■ Microwave: Not suitable.

RIGHT: Clockwise from top: Minced Lamb in Vine Leaves, Mussels in Herb and Caper Marinade, Deep-Fried Cheese and Anchovy Triangles.

MUSSELS IN TOMATO, WINE AND PARSLEY SAUCE

24 (about 1kg) large green-lipped
   mussels
2 tablespoons olive oil
1 leek, chopped
1 teaspoon dry mustard
1 tablespoon chopped fresh parsley
410g can tomatoes
1 tablespoon tomato paste
2 teaspoons plain flour
½ cup dry white wine

Scrub mussels, remove beards. Heat oil
in pan, add leek, mustard and parsley,
cook, stirring, until leek is soft. Add undrained crushed tomatoes, paste and
blended flour and wine, bring to boil, add
mussels, boil, covered, about 2 minutes.
Remove mussels from pan as they open.
Serve mussels with tomato, wine and
parsley sauce.

Serves 4.

■ Mussels best cooked just before
   serving.
■ Freeze: Not suitable.
■ Microwave: Suitable.

GNOCCHI WITH HAM AND CHEESE SAUCE

4 large (about 800g) potatoes, peeled,
   chopped
200g ricotta cheese
1¾ cups plain flour
3 cups milk
2 tablespoons chopped fresh parsley
2 cups water
1 tablespoon chopped fresh
   parsley, extra

HAM AND CHEESE SAUCE
40g butter
2 tablespoons plain flour
1 cup milk
¼ cup grated fresh parmesan cheese
1½ cups (185g) grated tasty cheese
1 teaspoon seeded mustard
1 (about 120g) ham steak, chopped

Boil, steam or microwave potatoes until
tender; drain. Push potatoes through
sieve into large bowl, add ricotta cheese,
mix well; gradually add sifted flour. Knead
dough on lightly floured surface until
smooth. Shape level teaspoons of mixture
into balls.

Place a ball in palm of hand, press
floured fork on top of dough to make indentations and to flatten slightly. Repeat
with remaining balls.

Combine milk, parsley and water in
large pan, bring to boil, add gnocchi in
batches, simmer, uncovered, about 5
minutes or until gnocchi rise to the surface
of the milk mixture.

Using slotted spoon, remove gnocchi
from pan, reserve cooking liquid for
sauce. Transfer gnocchi to serving dish
(6 cup capacity). Pour ham and cheese
sauce over gnocchi, serve sprinkled with
extra parsley.

Ham and Cheese Sauce: Melt butter in
pan, stir in flour, stir over heat until bubbling. Remove from heat, gradually stir in
2 cups of the reserved gnocchi cooking
liquid and the 1 cup milk, stir over heat
until mixture boils and thickens. Add
remaining ingredients, cook, stirring, until
heated through.

Serves 4.

■ Recipe best made close to serving.
■ Freeze: Not suitable.
■ Microwave: Sauce suitable.

GARLIC PRAWNS

750g uncooked prawns
½ cup olive oil
6 cloves garlic, crushed
1 small fresh red chilli, finely chopped
¼ cup chopped fresh parsley

Shell and devein prawns, leaving tails intact. Heat oil in pan, add garlic and chilli, cook, stirring, until chilli is soft. Add prawns, cook about 1 minute or until tender, turning once. Serve with garlic oil, sprinkled with parsley.

Serves 4.

■ Recipe best made just before serving.
■ Freeze: Not suitable.
■ Microwave: Not suitable.

FRIED CHEESE STICKS

2 cups (200g) grated kasseri cheese
2 tablespoons chopped fresh chives
3 eggs, lightly beaten
6 sheets fillo pastry
60g butter, melted
1 egg, lightly beaten, extra
oil for deep-frying

Combine cheese, chives and eggs in bowl. Layer 2 pastry sheets together, brushing each with butter. Cut layered sheets into 8 x 12cm x 14cm rectangles. Place 2 teaspoons cheese mixture on narrow end of pastry, roll end over, fold sides in, roll up, seal ends with extra egg,

Repeat with remaining pastry, butter, cheese mixture and extra egg.

Just before serving, deep-fry sticks in hot oil, until well browned, drain on absorbent paper, serve hot.

Makes 24.

■ Recipe can be prepared 6 hours ahead.
■ Storage: Covered, in refrigerator.
■ Freeze: Not suitable.
■ Microwave: Not suitable.

LEFT: From left: Gnocchi with Ham and Cheese Sauce, Mussels in Tomato, Wine and Parsley Sauce.
ABOVE: From top: Garlic Prawns, Fried Cheese Sticks.

Left: Plates from Villa Italiana; tiles from Pazotti
Above: Serving ware from Corso de Fiori

MINI PESTO PIZZAS WITH PRAWNS AND ARTICHOKES

12 (about 650g) cooked king prawns, shelled
12 bottled drained artichoke hearts, halved
1 cup (100g) grated mozzarella cheese

PIZZA BASES
15g compressed yeast
1 teaspoon sugar
¼ cup warm water
¼ cup warm milk
1 cup white plain flour
½ cup wholemeal plain flour
2 tablespoons olive oil

PESTO
2 tablespoons pine nuts, toasted
1 cup firmly packed basil leaves
1 clove garlic, crushed
2 tablespoons grated fresh parmesan cheese
⅓ cup olive oil

Spread pesto evenly over pizza bases; top with prawns and artichokes; sprinkle with cheese. Bake in moderately hot oven about 15 minutes or until pizzas are browned.
Pizza Bases: Cream yeast and sugar in small bowl; stir in water and milk, cover, stand in warm place about 10 minutes or until mixture is frothy.

Sift flours into large bowl, add yeast mixture and oil, mix to a firm dough. Turn dough onto floured surface, knead for about 5 minutes or until dough is smooth and elastic. Return dough to greased bowl, cover, stand in warm place about 1 hour or until dough is doubled in size.

Turn dough onto lightly floured surface, knead until smooth. Divide into 6 portions, roll each portion to a 10cm round. Place rounds onto lightly greased oven trays, shape sides to form pizza cases.
Pesto: Blend or process all ingredients until smooth.

Makes 6.

■ Pizzas best made close to serving.
■ Freeze: Suitable.
■ Microwave: Not suitable.

SPICED CARROT DIP

4 (about 500g) carrots, chopped
1½ cups water
½ large vegetable stock cube, crumbled
¼ cup olive oil
1 tablespoon white vinegar
1 clove garlic, crushed
¼ teaspoon ground oregano
¼ teaspoon paprika
¼ teaspoon ground cumin
1 red pepper, sliced
1 green pepper, sliced
black olives
flat bread

Combine carrots, water and stock cube in pan, bring to boil, simmer, covered, about 15 minutes or until carrots are tender, drain; discard stock. Place carrots in bowl, add combined oil, vinegar, garlic, oregano, paprika and cumin, cover; cool.

Blend or process carrot mixture until smooth. Serve dip with peppers, olives and bread.

Makes about 2½ cups.

■ Dip can be made a day ahead. Vegetables best prepared just before serving.
■ Storage: Dip, covered, in refrigerator.
■ Freeze: Not suitable.
■ Microwave: Suitable.

ANCHOVY TOASTS WITH GARLIC MAYONNAISE

1 small French bread stick
390g can pimientos, drained, finely sliced
fresh basil leaves
4 x 45g cans rolled anchovy fillets, drained

GARLIC MAYONNAISE
3 cloves garlic, crushed
2 teaspoons chopped fresh basil
2 egg yolks
1 teaspoon lemon juice
½ cup olive oil

Cut bread into ½cm (about 25) slices. Toast slices on oven tray in moderately slow oven about 15 minutes; cool. Spread toasts with garlic mayonnaise, top with pimientos, basil leaves and anchovies.
Garlic Mayonnaise: Blend or process garlic, basil, yolks and juice until smooth. While motor is operating, gradually add oil in a thin stream; process until thick.

Makes about 25.

■ Can be made an hour before serving.
■ Storage: Covered, in refrigerator.
■ Freeze: Not suitable.
■ Microwave: Not suitable.

LEFT: From top: Spiced Carrot Dip, Mini Pesto Pizzas with Prawns and Artichokes.
BELOW: Anchovy Toasts with Garlic Mayonnaise.

FRESH VEGETABLE STICKS WITH TAPENADE DIP

2 carrots
2 zucchini
1 red pepper
1 yellow pepper
125g snow peas

TAPENADE DIP
½ x 45g can drained anchovy fillets
1 tablespoon drained capers
12 pimiento-stuffed green olives
½ teaspoon seasoned pepper
⅓ cup olive oil
1 egg yolk

Cut carrots, zucchini and peppers into long strips. Trim snow peas. Add carrots and peas to pan of boiling water; drain immediately, rinse under cold water; drain well. Serve vegetable sticks with tapenade dip.

Tapenade Dip: Blend anchovies, capers, olives, seasoned pepper and 2 tablespoons of the oil until well combined. Add egg yolk, blend until just combined. Add remaining oil in thin stream while the motor is operating.

Serves 6.

■ Vegetables best prepared just before serving. Dip can be made a day ahead.
■ Storage: Dip, covered, in refrigerator.
■ Freeze: Not suitable.
■ Microwave: Vegetables suitable.

VINE LEAF AND BEEF ROLLS

40g butter
1 onion, chopped
2 cloves garlic, crushed
375g minced beef
410g can tomatoes
1½ tablespoons chopped
    fresh parsley
2 teaspoons chopped fresh oregano
½ cup cooked rice
200g packet vine leaves in brine,
    rinsed, drained
⅓ cup dry white wine
2 tablespoons lemon juice
2 cups boiling water
1 cup tomato puree
1 teaspoon sugar

Heat butter in pan, add onion and garlic, cook, stirring, until onion is soft. Add beef, cook, stirring, until well browned. Add undrained crushed tomatoes, parsley and oregano. Bring to boil, simmer, uncovered, about 5 minutes or until thick; stir in rice.

Place leaves smooth side down on board, place 2 level teaspoons of meat mixture onto each leaf, fold in sides, roll up to form parcels. Repeat with remaining leaves and mixture.

Place parcels in single layer in pan, pour over combined wine, juice, water and puree. Place upturned plate on top of parcels to prevent moving during cooking. Bring to boil, simmer, covered, about 45 minutes or until tender.

Remove rolls from sauce, add sugar to sauce, bring to boil, simmer, uncovered, about 3 minutes or until slightly thickened. Serve sauce with rolls.

Makes about 50.

■ Recipe can be made a day ahead.
■ Storage: Covered, in refrigerator.
■ Freeze: Not suitable.
■ Microwave: Suitable.

CHEESE AND SPINACH PASTRIES

30g butter
3 green shallots, chopped
½ bunch (20 leaves) English
    spinach, chopped
2 teaspoons chopped fresh dill
2 eggs, lightly beaten
125g feta cheese, grated
125g ricotta cheese
¼ teaspoon ground nutmeg
½ cup packaged breadcrumbs
10 sheets fillo pastry
75g butter, melted, extra

Heat butter in pan, add shallots, cook, stirring, until shallots are soft. Add spinach and dill, cook, stirring, about 3 minutes or until spinach is wilted; cool.

Squeeze excess liquid from spinach mixture, place spinach mixture in bowl. Add eggs, cheeses, nutmeg and breadcrumbs, mix well.

Layer 2 pastry sheets together, brushing each with some of the extra butter. Cut pastry crossways into 4 strips. Place 1 level tablespoon of spinach mixture at 1 end of each strip; fold in sides to enclose the filling.

To shape triangle, fold 1 end corner diagonally across to other edge to form a triangle. Continue folding to end of strip, maintaining triangular shape. Brush triangle with a little more extra butter. Repeat with remaining pastry, remaining extra butter and filling.

Just before serving, place triangles on lightly greased oven trays, bake in moderately hot oven about 15 minutes or until lightly browned and crisp.

Serves 6.

■ Triangles can be prepared 2 days ahead.
■ Storage: Covered, in refrigerator.
■ Freeze: Uncooked triangles suitable.
■ Microwave: Not suitable.

RIGHT: Clockwise from top left: Fresh Vegetable Sticks with Tapenade Dip, Cheese and Spinach Pastries, Vine Leaf and Beef Rolls.

Plates from Villa Italiana; tiles from Country Floors

EGGS FLAMENCA

We used white Hungarian garlic salami in this recipe.

2 (about 300g) potatoes
60g butter
6 slices (about 60g) smoked lean ham
1 onion, chopped
1 red pepper, chopped
150g frozen peas
150g green beans, sliced
½ bunch (6 spears) fresh asparagus, chopped
410g can tomatoes
2 tablespoons tomato paste
6 eggs
8 slices (about 30g) salami

Lightly grease 6 ovenproof dishes (1 cup capacity).

Peel and dice potatoes. Heat half the butter in pan, add potatoes, cook, stirring, until well browned. Remove potatoes from pan; drain on absorbent paper.

Chop half the ham. Heat remaining butter in pan, add chopped ham, onion and pepper, cook, stirring, until onion is soft. Add peas, beans and asparagus, cook, stirring, 2 minutes. Add undrained crushed tomatoes and paste. Bring to boil, simmer, uncovered, about 10 minutes or until slightly thickened, stir in potatoes.

Divide vegetable mixture between prepared dishes. Make a well in the centre of each mixture, carefully pour an egg into each hollow. Cut remaining ham and salami into squares, place around egg yolks. Bake, uncovered, in moderate oven about 15 minutes or until whites of eggs are set as desired.

Serves 6.

■ Recipe best made just before serving.
■ Freeze: Not suitable.
■ Microwave: Not suitable.

BELOW: Clockwise from top left: Eggs Flamenca, Mushroom and Pork Terrine, Marinated Octopus Salad.
RIGHT: Salmon Puffs.

Right: Plate from Villa Italiana

MARINATED OCTOPUS SALAD

2 bay leaves
1 onion, chopped
¼ cup fresh parsley sprigs, lightly
**   packed**
1 small fresh red chilli, halved
1 teaspoon black peppercorns
1 litre (4 cups) water
2kg baby octopus
1 tomato, chopped
1 onion, chopped, extra
2 cloves garlic, crushed
pinch ground saffron
¼ cup red wine vinegar
½ cup olive oil
1 tablespoon chopped fresh
**   parsley, extra**

Combine bay leaves, onion, parsley sprigs, chilli, peppercorns and water in large pan, bring to boil, simmer, covered, 15 minutes. Strain stock, discard onion and parsley mixture.

Remove and discard heads and beaks from octopus. Combine octopus and stock in pan, bring to boil, stirring, remove from heat. Stand pan, covered, until mixture is cooled to room temperature.

Blend or process tomato, extra onion, garlic, saffron, vinegar and oil until smooth, stir in chopped extra parsley.

Drain octopus from stock; discard stock. Combine octopus with tomato mixture in bowl, cover, refrigerate mixture before serving.

Serves 8.

■ Salad is best made 2 days
  before serving.
■ Storage: Covered, in refrigerator.
■ Freeze: Not suitable.
■ Microwave: Not suitable.

MUSHROOM AND PORK TERRINE

30g butter
1 tablespoon olive oil
4 green shallots, chopped
1 small onion, chopped
3 cloves garlic, crushed
3 bacon rashers, chopped
500g lambs' fry
300g pork and veal mince
1 tablespoon seeded mustard
½ cup stale breadcrumbs
1 tablespoon chopped fresh sage
2 tablespoons chopped fresh parsley
15 (about 200g) baby mushrooms

SAGE AND MUSTARD CREAM
1 tablespoon olive oil
1 green shallot, finely chopped
1 tablespoon chopped fresh sage
1 tablespoon seeded mustard
50g packaged cream cheese,
**   chopped**
¼ cup sour cream

Lightly grease 14cm x 21cm loaf pan. Heat butter and oil in pan, add shallots, onion, garlic and bacon, cook, stirring, until onion is soft. Blend or process lambs'

fry until finely minced, transfer to large bowl, add onion mixture, mince, mustard, breadcrumbs and herbs; mix well.

Press half the meat mixture into prepared pan. Remove stems from mushrooms, place mushrooms in single layer over meat mixture, top with remaining meat mixture; press down firmly.

Bake, covered, in moderate oven about 1 hour or until cooked through; cool. Drain excess liquid from terrine; refrigerate terrine until cold.

Just before serving, slice terrine, serve with sage and mustard cream.

Sage and Mustard Cream: Heat oil in pan, add shallot and sage, cook, stirring until shallot is soft. Add mustard, cheese and cream, stir over low heat until cheese has melted. Cool before using.

Serves 8.

■ Recipe can be made 3 days ahead.
■ Storage: Covered, in refrigerator.
■ Freeze: Not suitable.
■ Microwave: Cream suitable.

SALMON PUFFS

1 sheet ready-rolled puff pastry
1 egg yolk
250g Atlantic salmon fillet
¼ cup lemon juice
2 medium fresh red chillies, finely
**   chopped**
¼ teaspoon paprika
2 teaspoons chopped fresh tarragon
2 baby onions, thinly sliced
2 medium fresh red chillies, thinly
**   sliced, extra**

Cut pastry into 36 x 4cm squares. Place squares on oven trays, prick well with fork, brush lightly with egg yolk. Bake in hot oven about 8 minutes or until browned and puffed; cool on trays.

Place salmon in pan, cover with water, bring to boil, simmer, uncovered, until just tender; drain, remove skin. Place salmon in shallow dish, pour over juice, chopped chilli, paprika and tarragon, cover, refrigerate several hours or overnight.

Just before serving, drain salmon, cut into 36 pieces. Top pastry squares with salmon, onion and extra sliced chillies.

Makes 36.

■ Pastry and salmon can be prepared a
  day ahead.
■ Storage: Pastry, in airtight container.
  Salmon, covered, in refrigerator.
■ Freeze: Pastry suitable.
■ Microwave: Not suitable.

over heat until liquid has evaporated.

Melt extra butter in pan, stir in flour, stir over heat until bubbling. Remove from heat, gradually stir in 1 cup of the reserved stock and cream, stir over heat until mixture boils and thickens. Add seafood, dill and mushrooms; mix well.

Serves 4.

■ Crepes and sauce can be prepared a day ahead.
■ Storage: Crepes, layered with greaseproof paper and covered, in refrigerator. Sauce, covered, in refrigerator.
■ Freeze: Crepes suitable.
■ Microwave: Suitable.

VEAL, HAM AND CHICKEN TERRINE

500g veal steaks, chopped
100g ham, chopped
250g chicken breast fillets
20g butter
1 onion, chopped
2 cloves garlic, crushed
¼ cup canned drained chopped pimientos
2 teaspoons chopped fresh rosemary
2 teaspoons canned drained green peppercorns, crushed
2 eggs, lightly beaten
1 cup stale breadcrumbs
1 small chicken stock cube, crumbled

Grease 14cm x 21cm loaf pan, line base with paper, grease paper. Process veal and ham until combined. Cut chicken into 1cm cubes. Heat butter in pan, add onion and garlic, cook, stirring, until onion is soft.

Combine veal mixture, chicken, onion mixture, pimientos, rosemary, peppercorns, eggs, breadcrumbs and stock cube; mix well.

Spread mixture into prepared pan, cover with greased foil, place in baking dish with enough boiling water to come halfway up sides of pan. Bake in moderate oven about 1¼ hours or until cooked through; cool in pan.

Drain excess liquid from terrine, turn out, cover, refrigerate. Slice when cold.

Serves 8.

■ Terrine can be made a day ahead.
■ Storage: Covered, in refrigerator.
■ Freeze: Not suitable.
■ Microwave: Not suitable.

SEAFOOD CREPES

¾ cup plain flour
3 eggs, lightly beaten
1 tablespoon oil
1 cup milk
butter
½ cup grated tasty cheese
pinch paprika

FILLING
1¼ cups water
½ cup dry white wine
1 small chicken stock cube, crumbled
150g white fish fillet, chopped
125g scallops
20g butter
100g mushrooms, chopped
1 tablespoon lemon juice
45g butter, extra
¼ cup plain flour
¼ cup cream
2 teaspoons chopped fresh dill
125g cooked shelled school prawns

Sift flour into bowl, add combined eggs, oil and milk, slowly whisk liquid into flour until batter is smooth. Strain into jug.

Heat pan, add small knob of butter, swirl butter evenly around pan. Pour 2 to 3 tablespoons of batter into pan, swirl to cover base of pan evenly. Cook until lightly browned underneath, turn crepe, brown other side. Repeat with remaining batter. You will need 8 crepes for this recipe.

Divide filling between crepes, roll crepes. Place crepes seam-side-down in single layer in greased ovenproof dish, sprinkle with cheese and paprika. Bake, uncovered, in moderate oven about 15 minutes or until cheese has melted and crepes are heated through.

Filling: Heat water, wine and stock cube in pan, add fish and scallops, simmer, uncovered, until tender; drain on absorbent paper; reserve stock.

Heat butter in pan, add mushrooms, cook, stirring, until tender. Stir in juice, stir

ABOVE LEFT: From top: Veal, Ham and Chicken Terrine, Seafood Crepes.
ABOVE RIGHT: From top: Eggplant Dip, Pickled Vegetable Antipasto.

Above: Plates and glass from Corso de Fiori

PICKLED VEGETABLE ANTIPASTO

¼ small (about 150g) cauliflower
2 carrots
1 red pepper
1 green pepper
100g okra
25 (about 700g) pickling onions
20 black olives
1 radicchio lettuce
120g csabai salami, sliced
250g black olives, extra

PICKLING VINEGAR
4½ cups white vinegar
2 teaspoons white mustard seeds
1 teaspoon turmeric
1 teaspoon garam masala
4 bay leaves
12 black peppercorns
2 small fresh red chillies

Cut cauliflower into small pieces. Cut carrots and peppers into 1cm x 5cm strips.

Cook cauliflower, carrots, peppers, okra and onions in large pan of boiling water about 2 minutes or until vegetables are just tender; drain.

Place hot vegetables and olives in sterilised jars. Pour pickling vinegar over the vegetables, seal and stand 1 week before using.

Serve pickled vegetables with radicchio lettuce, salami and extra olives.

Pickling Vinegar: Combine vinegar, seeds, turmeric, garam masala, bay leaves, peppercorns and whole chillies in large jug.

Serves 6.

■ Storage: Covered, in refrigerator.
■ Freeze: Not suitable.
■ Microwave: Not suitable.

EGGPLANT DIP

2 x 500g eggplants
1 clove garlic, crushed
1 small onion, grated
⅓ cup chopped fresh parsley
2 tablespoons olive oil
2 tablespoons lemon juice

Bake whole unpeeled eggplants in moderate oven about 1¼ hours or until tender; cool slightly, peel and chop. Blend or process eggplants, garlic, onion, parsley, oil and juice until smooth. Refrigerate dip until cold. Serve with fresh vegetables and crackers.

Makes about 3 cups.

■ Dip can be made 2 days ahead.
■ Storage: Covered, in refrigerator.
■ Freeze: Not suitable.
■ Microwave: Not suitable.

TOMATO, PEPPER AND HAM OMELETTES

1 red pepper
30g butter
1 red Spanish onion, chopped
1 clove garlic, crushed
100g ham, chopped
2 (about 250g) tomatoes, peeled, chopped
½ teaspoon cracked black peppercorns
1 tablespoon chopped fresh chives
6 eggs, lightly beaten

Quarter pepper, remove seeds and membrane. Grill pepper, skin side up, until skin blisters and blackens. Peel skin from pepper, chop pepper.

Heat butter in pan, add onion, garlic and ham, cook, stirring, until onion is soft. Add red pepper, tomatoes and chives; cool. Drain excess liquid; discard liquid.

Combine ham mixture and eggs in bowl, mix well. Pour half the mixture into lightly greased heated non-stick omelette pan, cook, without stirring, until omelette is almost set and browned underneath. Fold in half and continue to cook until egg mixture is set. Repeat with remaining mixture. Cut each omelette in half before serving.

Serves 4.

■ Omelette is best made close to serving.
■ Freeze: Not suitable.
■ Microwave: Not suitable.

PORK AND PROSCIUTTO ROLLS IN GARLIC CRUMBS

300g pork fillet
150g prosciutto
1 egg, lightly beaten
2 tablespoons milk
1½ cups (100g) stale breadcrumbs
1 teaspoon garlic powder
1 tablespoon chopped fresh parsley
oil for deep-frying

SAUCE
60g butter
¼ cup plain flour
1 cup milk
½ cup water
1 small chicken stock cube, crumbled

Cut pork into thin slices down the length of fillet. Using flat blade of knife, run blade along slices to flatten. Cut each slice into 3cm x 6cm strips. Cut prosciutto into 3cm x 6cm strips.

Place a strip of prosciutto on each slice of pork, roll up and secure with toothpicks. Dip rolls in warm sauce to coat completely. Place rolls in single layer on foil-covered tray, refrigerate several hours or until sauce is set.

Dip rolls in combined egg and milk, then into combined breadcrumbs, garlic and parsley, press crumbs on firmly.

Just before serving, deep-fry rolls in hot oil until well browned and cooked through; drain on absorbent paper.

Sauce: Melt butter in small pan, stir in flour, stir over heat until bubbling. Remove from heat, gradually stir in milk, water and stock cube, stir over heat until sauce boils and thickens.

Makes about 40.

■ Recipe can be prepared a day ahead.
■ Storage: Covered, in refrigerator.
■ Freeze: Not suitable.
■ Microwave: Not suitable.

SPICY VEAL AND TOMATO TURNOVERS

4 sheets ready-rolled puff pastry
1 egg, lightly beaten
½ teaspoon caraway seeds

FILLING
150g stewing veal, chopped
1 tablespoon olive oil
1 onion, chopped
1 clove garlic, crushed
100g csabai salami, chopped
390g can pimientos, drained, chopped
¼ cup tomato paste
¼ cup dry white wine
1 teaspoon cracked black peppercorns
2 tablespoons chopped fresh parsley
8 pimiento-stuffed green olives, chopped

Cut pastry into 16 x 11cm rounds. Divide filling evenly between each round. Fold pastry over to enclose filling, press edges together with fork.

Place turnovers on lightly greased oven trays, brush turnovers with egg, sprinkle with seeds. Bake in moderately hot oven about 15 minutes or until pastry is puffed and lightly browned.

Filling: Blend or process veal until finely minced. Heat oil in pan, add onion and garlic, cook, stirring, until onion is soft. Add veal and salami, cook further 5 minutes or until veal is well browned. Add pimientos, paste and wine, bring to boil, simmer, uncovered, about 2 minutes or until liquid has evaporated. Stir in peppercorns, parsley and olives; cool.

Serves 8.

■ Filling can be made a day ahead.
■ Storage: Covered, in refrigerator.
■ Freeze: Uncooked turnovers suitable.
■ Microwave: Not suitable.

RIGHT: Clockwise from top left: Spicy Veal and Tomato Turnovers, Tomato, Pepper and Ham Omelette, Pork and Prosciutto Rolls in Garlic Crumbs.

Plates from Villa Italiana; tiles from Pazotti

GARLIC PORK KEBABS WITH MUSHROOM BUTTER SAUCE

700g pork fillets, chopped
1¼ cups olive oil
1 cup white vinegar
12 cloves garlic, crushed
6 small fresh red chillies, chopped
1 teaspoon paprika
3 bay leaves
80g butter
300g baby mushrooms, quartered

Thread pork onto 18 skewers; place kebabs in shallow dish. Combine 1 cup of the oil, vinegar, garlic, chillies, paprika and bay leaves in bowl, pour marinade over kebabs, cover tightly, refrigerate several hours or overnight.

Just before serving, drain kebabs, discard marinade. Heat remaining oil in pan, cook kebabs in batches until browned all over and tender; keep warm. Add butter and mushrooms to pan, cook, stirring, until mushrooms are tender. Serve kebabs with butter mushroom sauce.

Serves 6.

■ Kebabs can be prepared 2 days ahead.
■ Storage: Covered, in refrigerator.
■ Freeze: Kebabs suitable.
■ Microwave: Not suitable.

CUCUMBER, YOGURT AND GARLIC DIP

2 small green cucumbers, finely grated
500g plain yogurt
3 cloves garlic, crushed
2 green shallots, finely chopped
1 tablespoon chopped fresh parsley

Squeeze cucumbers well to remove excess moisture. Combine cucumbers with remaining ingredients in bowl; mix well. Refrigerate dip 2 hours before serving.

Makes about 2 cups.

■ Dip can be prepared a day ahead.
■ Storage: Covered, in refrigerator.
■ Freeze: Not suitable.
■ Microwave: Not suitable.

OMELETTE STACK WITH FRESH HERB DRESSING

¼ **bunch (10 leaves) English spinach**
9 **eggs, lightly beaten**
1 **onion, grated**
14 **black olives, finely chopped**
¼ **cup chopped pimientos**
3 **teaspoons butter**
1 **cup (125g) grated tasty cheese**

HERB DRESSING
¼ **cup olive oil**
1 **tablespoon red wine vinegar**
1 **teaspoon seeded mustard**
1 **tablespoon chopped fresh mint**
1 **tablespoon chopped fresh chives**

Steam or microwave spinach until just wilted; drain well.

Combine eggs and onion in bowl; mix well. Divide mixture evenly into 3 bowls.

Pat dry spinach, olives and pimientos between layers of absorbent paper. Add spinach to 1 bowl of egg mixture, add olives to another bowl and pimientos to remaining bowl. Blend or process each mixture separately until almost smooth.

Heat 1 teaspoon of the butter in heavy-based crepe pan, pour in olive mixture. Cook over heat, without stirring, 3 minutes. Place pan under hot griller about 1 minute or until omelette is lightly browned. Lift olive omelette onto serving plate, sprinkle with half the cheese.

Repeat process with remaining butter, pimiento mixture and spinach mixture.

Place pimiento omelette over cheese layer, sprinkle with remaining cheese, top with spinach omelette. Cut omelette stack into wedges, serve with herb dressing.

Herb Dressing: Combine all ingredients in jar, shake well.

Serves 8.

■ Recipe best made just before serving.
■ Freeze: Not suitable.
■ Microwave: Not suitable.

SEAFOOD SOUFFLES WITH LEMON CAPER SAUCE

¼ **cup grated fresh parmesan cheese**
40g **butter**
⅓ **cup plain flour**
1 **cup milk**
250g **white fish fillets, chopped**
3 **eggs, separated**
2 **tablespoons chopped fresh chives**
½ **cup grated Swiss cheese**
250g **small cooked prawns, shelled**

LEMON CAPER SAUCE
¼ **cup lemon juice**
2 **green shallots, chopped**
2 **tablespoons dry white wine**
1 **tablespoon water**
1 **cup cream**
15g **butter**
3 **teaspoons plain flour**
1 **tablespoon drained capers**
2 **teaspoons chopped fresh dill**

Grease 4 ovenproof dishes (1 cup capacity), sprinkle dishes with parmesan cheese; place dishes on oven tray.

Melt butter in pan, stir in flour, stir over heat until bubbling. Remove from heat, gradually stir in milk, stir over heat until mixture boils and thickens. Process fish until finely minced.

Combine sauce, fish, egg yolks, chives and Swiss cheese in bowl. Beat egg whites in small bowl with electric mixer until soft peaks form, fold into fish mixture in 2 batches.

Spoon half the souffle mixture into prepared dishes, top with prawns, spoon remaining souffle mixture over prawns. Bake in moderately hot oven about 30 minutes or until puffed and well browned. Serve with lemon caper sauce.

Lemon Caper Sauce: Combine juice, shallots, wine and water in pan, bring to boil, simmer, uncovered, 2 minutes; strain, discard shallots. Return liquid to pan, add cream, bring to boil, add blended butter and flour, cook, stirring, over heat until mixture boils and thickens, stir in capers and dill.

Serves 4.

■ Souffles best made just before serving. Sauce can be made 3 hours ahead.
■ Storage: Sauce, covered, in refrigerator.
■ Freeze: Not suitable.
■ Microwave: Sauce suitable.

LEFT: Clockwise from top: Garlic Pork Kebabs with Mushroom Butter Sauce, Cucumber, Yogurt and Garlic Dip, Omelette Stack with Fresh Herb Dressing.
BELOW: Seafood Souffle with Lemon Caper Sauce.

FRESH TOMATO AND EGGPLANT PASTA

1 (about 300g) eggplant
coarse cooking salt
oil for deep-frying
2 tablespoons olive oil
1 onion, chopped
2 cloves garlic, crushed
4 large (about 1kg) ripe tomatoes,
**   peeled, chopped**
2 cups (180g) penne pasta
2 tablespoons shredded fresh basil

Cut eggplant in half lengthways, cut each half into thick slices, place in bowl, sprinkle with salt, stand 20 minutes. Rinse eggplant under cold water, pat dry with absorbent paper.

Deep-fry eggplant in batches in hot oil until lightly browned, drain on absorbent paper.

Heat olive oil in pan, add onion and garlic, cook, stirring, until onion is soft. Add tomatoes, simmer, uncovered, about 25 minutes or until all liquid has evaporated, stirring occasionally.

Add pasta to large pan of boiling water, boil, uncovered, until just tender; drain.

Just before serving, combine eggplant, sauce, pasta and basil; serve hot.

Serves 4.

■ Recipe can be prepared 2 hours ahead.
■ Storage: Covered, at room temperature.
■ Freeze: Not suitable.
■ Microwave: Pasta suitable.

HERBED EGGPLANT SLICE

2 x 500g eggplants, thinly sliced
coarse cooking salt
⅔ cup olive oil
1 red pepper
3 cloves garlic, crushed
1½ tablespoons chopped fresh
**   rosemary**
1 tablespoon chopped fresh oregano
1 cup (80g) grated fresh parmesan
**   cheese**

Lightly grease shallow 20cm x 32cm ovenproof dish. Place eggplant slices in bowl, sprinkle with salt, stand 20 minutes. Rinse eggplant under cold water, pat dry with absorbent paper. Heat oil in pan, add eggplant in single layer, cook until well browned; drain on absorbent paper.

Quarter pepper, remove seeds and membrane. Grill pepper, skin side up, until skin blisters and blackens. Peel skin, cut pepper into thin strips.

Place a third of the eggplant slices into prepared dish, sprinkle with a third of the combined garlic, rosemary and oregano. Repeat layering, ending with herbs. Sprinkle slice with cheese. Bake, uncovered, in moderate oven about 20 minutes or until cheese is melted and lightly browned. Cut slice into 8 squares, layer squares together. Serve topped with red pepper.

Serves 4.

■ Recipe can be prepared 3 hours ahead.
■ Storage: Covered, in refrigerator.
■ Freeze: Not suitable.
■ Microwave: Not suitable.

LEFT: From top: Herbed Eggplant Slice, Fresh Tomato and Eggplant Pasta.

ABOVE: Herb and Pine Nut Pie with Tomato Coulis.

Left: Plates from Villa Italiana; tiles from Country Floors

HERB AND PINE NUT PIE WITH TOMATO COULIS

1 bunch (40 leaves) English spinach
1 small leek, chopped
⅓ cup pine nuts
2 tablespoons chopped fresh chives
1 tablespoon chopped fresh thyme
1 tablespoon chopped fresh basil
3 eggs, lightly beaten
100g gruyere cheese, chopped
2 tablespoons grated fresh parmesan cheese
½ teaspoon cracked black peppercorns
⅓ cup packaged breadcrumbs
2 tablespoons sesame seeds
1 egg, lightly beaten, extra

PASTRY
2¼ cups plain flour
180g butter
2 eggs, lightly beaten

TOMATO COULIS
1 tablespoon olive oil
4 large (about 1kg) ripe tomatoes, chopped
½ cup tomato puree
1 onion, grated
1 fresh thyme sprig
1 bay leaf
1 teaspoon sugar

Steam or microwave spinach until wilted; drain. Squeeze spinach to remove excess liquid; chop spinach finely.

Combine spinach, leek, nuts, herbs, eggs, cheeses, peppercorns and breadcrumbs; mix well. Lightly grease oven tray, sprinkle with half the sesame seeds. Cut pastry in half, roll out half between sheets of greaseproof paper to 23cm circle, place on seeds on oven tray. Spoon filling onto centre of pastry leaving 2cm border; brush border with a little water.

Roll out remaining pastry between sheets of greaseproof paper into 25cm circle, place over filling; pinch pastry edges together to seal. Brush pie with extra egg, sprinkle with remaining seeds.
Just before serving, bake pie in moderately hot oven about 40 minutes or until well browned and cooked through. Stand 5 minutes before serving. Serve hot with tomato coulis.

Pastry: Sift flour into bowl, rub in butter, add eggs; mix to a soft dough. Press dough into ball, knead gently on lightly floured surface until smooth, cover, refrigerate 30 minutes.

Tomato Coulis: Heat oil in pan, add remaining ingredients, cook, uncovered 40 minutes. Push mixture through sieve, discard pulp, return liquid to pan, bring to the boil, simmer, uncovered, about 20 minutes or until coulis thickens slightly.

Serves 8.

■ Uncooked pie can be made 3 hours ahead. Coulis can be made 2 days ahead.
■ Storage: Both, covered, in refrigerator.
■ Freeze: Uncooked pie suitable.
■ Microwave: Filling suitable.

GOATS' CHEESE WRAPPED IN TAPENADE

400g goats' cheese
100g packaged cream cheese, softened
45g can anchovy fillets, drained, finely chopped
⅓ cup drained sun-dried tomatoes, finely chopped
2 tablespoons drained capers, finely chopped

TAPENADE
396g can pitted black olives, drained
1 clove garlic, crushed
2 teaspoons seeded mustard
1 teaspoon lemon juice
1 bay leaf
2 tablespoons chopped fresh basil
2 tablespoons olive oil
2 cups stale breadcrumbs

DRESSING
2 tablespoons French mustard
2 tablespoons white vinegar
2 cloves garlic, crushed
2 cups olive oil
1 small red pepper, finely chopped

Combine cheeses in bowl; mix well. Place 30cm x 40cm sheet of foil on bench, top with a sheet of plastic wrap. Spread cheese mixture into 30cm x 35cm rectangle on plastic. Sprinkle anchovies, tomatoes and capers along long side of rectangle, roll up like a Swiss roll, twist ends of foil; refrigerate roll until firm.

On another 30cm x 40cm sheet of foil, spread tapenade into 30cm x 35cm rectangle. Carefully unwrap cheese roll, place on long side of tapenade, roll tapenade around cheese roll, twist ends of foil, refrigerate several hours or overnight.

Just before serving, unwrap roll, serve cut into 1½cm slices with dressing.

Tapenade: Blend or process olives, garlic, mustard, juice, bay leaf and basil. While motor is operating add oil gradually, transfer mixture to bowl, add breadcrumbs; mix well.

Dressing: Combine mustard, vinegar, garlic and oil in bowl, add pepper; mix well.

Serves 8.

- Roll can be made 2 days ahead.
- Storage: Covered, in refrigerator.
- Freeze: Not suitable.
- Microwave: Not suitable.

MEATBALLS IN EGG AND LEMON SAUCE

500g minced beef
½ cup rice
½ teaspoon ground cumin
⅓ cup chopped fresh parsley
50g butter, melted
cornflour
1 litre (4 cups) water
1 small beef stock cube, crumbled
1 egg
1 egg yolk
¼ cup lemon juice

Combine mince, rice, cumin, parsley and butter in bowl; mix well. Roll level tablespoons of mixture into balls, toss in cornflour, shake away excess cornflour.

Combine water and stock cube in large pan, bring to boil, add meatballs to stock, simmer, covered, about 20 minutes or until meatballs are tender.

Just before serving, beat egg and egg yolk in small bowl until thick and creamy, gradually add juice and ½ cup hot stock. Add egg mixture to meatball mixture, stirring gently to coat meatballs. Cook, uncovered, without boiling, until heated through. Discard remaining stock.

Serves 6.

- Recipe can be prepared 2 hours ahead.
- Storage: Covered, at room temperature.
- Freeze: Not suitable.
- Microwave: Not suitable.

CSABAI PUFFS WITH COOL CHILLI SAUCE

1 cup plain flour
¼ teaspoon turmeric
¼ teaspoon chilli powder
1 small beef stock cube, crumbled
2 eggs, separated
2 tablespoons olive oil
½ cup water
200g csabai salami, finely chopped
½ small red pepper, finely chopped
oil for deep-frying

COOL CHILLI SAUCE
½ cup plain yogurt
½ cup sour cream
1½ teaspoons white vinegar
1 small fresh red chilli, finely chopped
3 green shallots, chopped

Sift flour, spices and stock cube into bowl; stir in combined egg yolks, oil and water (or blend or process flour, spices, stock cube, egg yolks, oil and water until smooth). Stir in salami and pepper, cover, stand 30 minutes.

Beat egg whites in small bowl until soft peaks form; fold into salami mixture. Deep-fry ½ tablespoons of mixture in hot oil in batches until browned; drain on absorbent paper. Serve with cool chilli sauce.

Cool Chilli Sauce: Combine all ingredients in bowl, cover, refrigerate several hours or overnight.

Makes about 40.

■ Batter can be prepared 1 hour ahead.
  Sauce can be prepared a day ahead.
■ Storage: Both, covered, in refrigerator.
■ Freeze: Not suitable.
■ Microwave: Not suitable.

LEFT: Goats' Cheese Wrapped in Tapenade.
ABOVE: Clockwise from top: Meatballs in
Egg and Lemon Sauce, Csabai Puffs with
Cool Chilli Sauce, Prawn Pancakes.

PRAWN PANCAKES

2 tablespoons olive oil
1 small onion, finely chopped
2 tablespoons chopped fresh parsley
pinch paprika
2 eggs
½ cup plain flour
⅓ cup water
250g cooked shelled prawns,
    finely chopped
2 tablespoons olive oil, extra

Heat oil in pan, add onion, parsley and
paprika, cook, stirring, until onion is soft;
cool. Whisk eggs in bowl, gradually whisk

in sifted flour and water; beat until smooth
(or blend or process eggs, flour and water
until smooth). Add onion mixture and
prawns to batter; mix well.
Just before serving, heat extra oil in pan,
cook level tablespoons of mixture about
1 minute on each side or until well
browned. Drain on absorbent paper.

Makes about 24.

■ Recipe can be prepared 4 hours
  ahead.
■ Storage: Covered, in refrigerator.
■ Freeze: Not suitable.
■ Microwave: Not suitable.

POULTRY & RABBIT

There's a delicious sense of adventure when you combine flavours that may not be familiar. Our rabbit casseroles are superb: one with olives and capers, and another with herb-kissed red wine sauce. Chicken has fresh zest when roasted with pork and olive seasoning, or with a light fig compote, or in ginger and saffron sauce garnished with eggs and almonds. And if you've never tried duck breast fillets, you'll find preparation easy with our photographs. There are pick-up-and-eat drumsticks, quick quail and spatchcocks and − as a tasty contrast − rice and chicken liver patties or chicken and smoked ham balls.

GINGER SAFFRON CHICKEN WITH EGGS AND ALMONDS

40g butter
1 large onion, chopped
2 tablespoons chopped fresh parsley
½ teaspoon ground ginger
pinch ground saffron
8 chicken thighs
1 litre (4 cups) water
2 teaspoons cornflour
2 teaspoons lemon juice
4 hard-boiled eggs, quartered
½ cup blanched almonds, toasted

Heat butter in pan, add onion, parsley, ginger and saffron, cook, stirring, until onion is soft. Add chicken and water, bring to boil, simmer, uncovered, about 30 minutes or until chicken is tender. Remove chicken from pan; keep warm.

Boil liquid until reduced to about 2 cups. Stir in blended cornflour and juice, cook, stirring, until sauce boils and thickens. Serve chicken topped with sauce, eggs and almonds.

Serves 4.

■ Recipe can be prepared 2 hours ahead.
■ Storage: Covered, in refrigerator.
■ Freeze: Not suitable.
■ Microwave: Not suitable.

PORK AND OLIVE SEASONED CHICKEN

1 tablespoon olive oil
1 red Spanish onion, chopped
2 cloves garlic, crushed
200g pork fillet, chopped
100g csabai salami, chopped
100g chicken livers, chopped
100g pimiento-stuffed green olives, halved
1.5kg chicken
plain flour
2 tablespoons olive oil, extra
¼ cup water

Heat oil in pan, add onion and garlic, cook, stirring until onion is soft. Add pork and salami, cook, stirring, about 5 minutes or until pork is well browned and tender. Add livers, cook, stirring, further 1 minute; stir in olives.

Fill chicken with pork and olive mixture. Tie legs together, tuck wings under body, secure openings with skewers.

Coat chicken with flour, shake away excess flour.

Heat extra oil in large deep pan, add chicken, cook until well browned all over. Add water, simmer, covered, about 1¼ hours or until chicken is tender. Remove chicken from pan, keep warm. Strain pan juices, skim off fat, return juices to pan, bring to boil; serve with chicken.

Serves 6.

■ Recipe can be made a day ahead.
■ Storage: Covered, in refrigerator.
■ Freeze: Not suitable.
■ Microwave: Not suitable.

CHICKEN WITH ROSEMARY AND ONIONS

60g butter
2 tablespoons olive oil
4 chicken breast fillets
4 cloves garlic, crushed
2 tablespoons chopped fresh rosemary
1 teaspoon cracked black peppercorns
2 onions, chopped
1 cup dry white wine

Heat butter and oil in pan, add chicken, cook until well browned all over; remove from pan. Add garlic, rosemary, peppercorns and onions to pan, cook, stirring, until onions are soft. Return chicken to pan, add wine, bring to boil, simmer, covered, about 20 minutes or until chicken is tender.

Remove chicken from pan, keep warm. Bring onion mixture to boil, simmer, uncovered, until most of the liquid has evaporated. Serve onion mixture with warm chicken.

Serves 4.

■ Recipe is best made close to serving.
■ Freeze: Suitable.
■ Microwave: Not suitable.

RIGHT: Clockwise from top left: Pork and Olive Seasoned Chicken, Chicken with Rosemary and Onions, Ginger Saffron Chicken with Eggs and Almonds.

Platter from Accoutrement; tiles from Country Floors

ROAST QUAIL WITH POLENTA

2 leeks, sliced
8 quail
2 cloves garlic, crushed
1 onion, chopped
2 large tomatoes, peeled, chopped
1 cup water
1 small chicken stock cube, crumbled
½ cup dry red wine
1 tablespoon tomato paste

POLENTA
1 litre (4 cups) water
**2 small chicken stock cubes,
    crumbled**
1 cup polenta
1 tablespoon olive oil
¼ cup chopped fresh parsley

Divide leeks between quail cavities, tie legs together. Place quail in greased baking dish, bake, uncovered, in moderate oven about 35 minutes or until tender. Remove quail from baking dish; keep warm.

Place baking dish on stove, add garlic and onion, cook, stirring, until onion is soft. Add tomatoes, water, stock cube, wine and paste, bring to boil, simmer, uncovered 10 minutes. Blend or process sauce until smooth.

Just before serving, cut polenta into squares, place on oven tray, heat in moderate oven about 10 minutes. Serve quail with polenta and sauce.

Polenta: Combine water and stock cubes in pan, bring to boil, gradually add polenta, oil and parsley, stir over heat about 5 minutes or until mixture is thick. Pour mixture into greased 20cm x 30cm lamington pan; cool to room temperature.

Serves 8.

■ Polenta can be made a day ahead.
■ Storage: Covered, in refrigerator.
■ Freeze: Not suitable.
■ Microwave: Not suitable.

CHICKEN SAUTE WITH SALAMI AND BABY ONIONS

1 tablespoon olive oil
8 chicken thigh fillets, halved
8 baby onions
½ cup marsala
½ cup tomato puree
1 small chicken stock cube, crumbled
**¼ teaspoon cracked black
    peppercorns**
**10 slices (about 80g) calabrese
    salami, chopped**
**1½ tablespoons chopped fresh
    parsley**

Heat oil in pan, add chicken and onions, cook until chicken is well browned all over. Add marsala, bring to boil, simmer, uncovered, until wine is reduced by half. Add puree, stock cube and peppercorns, simmer, covered about 20 minutes or until chicken is tender. Stir in salami and parsley just before serving.

Serves 4 to 6.

■ Recipe can be made a day ahead.
■ Storage: Covered, in refrigerator.
■ Freeze: Suitable.
■ Microwave: Not suitable.

GRILLED SPATCHCOCKS WITH PESTO AND SALAD

4 x 400g spatchcocks

PESTO
1 cup firmly packed fresh basil leaves
⅔ cup olive oil
½ cup grated fresh parmesan cheese
3 cloves garlic, crushed
2 tablespoons pine nuts

SALAD
1 bunch endive
1 red pepper, sliced
½ cup cider vinegar
2 tablespoons olive oil
¼ cup chopped fresh chives

Cut spatchcocks into quarters. Combine spatchcocks and half the pesto in bowl, cover, refrigerate overnight. Reserve remaining pesto, cover; refrigerate.

Just before serving, grill spatchcocks until tender. Serve spatchcocks on salad, topped with reserved pesto.

Pesto: Blend or process all ingredients until smooth.

Salad: Tear endive into pieces. Combine all ingredients in bowl.

Serves 8.

■ Spatchcocks and pesto can be prepared 2 days ahead.
■ Storage: Covered, in refrigerator.
■ Freeze: Pesto suitable.
■ Microwave: Not suitable.

LEFT: From left: Roast Quail with Polenta, Chicken Saute with Salami and Baby Onions. ABOVE: Grilled Spatchcocks with Pesto and Salad.

Above: Bowl and rug from Corso de Fiori

RICE AND CHICKEN LIVER PATTIES

1 tablespoon olive oil
300g chicken livers, finely chopped
2 teaspoons chopped fresh
    thyme leaves
2 tablespoons dry red wine
45g butter
1 onion, finely chopped
1½ cups rice
1 bay leaf
3 cups water
3 small chicken stock cubes,
    crumbled
1 cup (80g) grated fresh parmesan
    cheese
3 eggs, lightly beaten
¼ cup chopped fresh parsley
plain flour
1 egg, lightly beaten, extra
2 tablespoons milk
1 cup packaged breadcrumbs,
    approximately
oil for shallow-frying

SAUTEED VEGETABLES
1 large (500g) eggplant, sliced
1 onion, sliced
1 red pepper, sliced
coarse cooking salt
2 tablespoons olive oil
1 clove garlic, crushed

Heat oil in pan, add livers and thyme, cook, stirring, until livers are tender. Add wine, simmer 1 minute.

Melt butter in pan, add onion, cook, stirring, until onion is soft. Add rice, bay leaf, water and stock cubes, bring to boil, simmer, covered, about 20 minutes or until most of the liquid is absorbed. Remove rice from heat, stir in liver mixture, cheese, eggs and parsley, cool, cover, refrigerate.

Divide mixture into 16 portions, shape into patties. Coat patties with flour, shake away excess flour, dip patties in combined extra egg and milk, then breadcrumbs; place on tray, refrigerate 30 minutes.

Shallow-fry patties in hot oil about 5 minutes on each side or until well browned; drain on absorbent paper. Serve patties on sauteed vegetables.

Sauteed Vegetables: Sprinkle vegetables with salt in bowl, stand 30 minutes, rinse under cold water; drain. Heat oil in pan, add garlic and vegetables, cook, stirring, until soft.

Serves 8.

■ Patties can be prepared 2 days ahead. Vegetables best made just before serving.
■ Storage: Patties, covered, in refrigerator.
■ Freeze: Patties suitable.
■ Microwave: Not suitable.

HONEYED SPATCHCOCKS WITH GLAZED GARLIC PEPPERS

½ cup olive oil
80g butter, melted
⅓ cup red wine vinegar
1 tablespoon ground cumin
1 teaspoon cumin seeds
⅔ cup honey
4 x 400g spatchcocks

GLAZED GARLIC PEPPERS
12 cloves garlic
60g butter
1½ tablespoons olive oil
½ cup red wine vinegar
1 small red pepper, finely sliced
1 small yellow pepper, finely sliced
¼ cup honey

Pour combined oil, butter, vinegar, cumin, seeds and honey over spatchcocks; cover, refrigerate several hours or overnight, turning occasionally.

Just before serving, drain spatchcocks; reserve marinade. Place spatchcocks on wire rack in baking dish, bake, uncovered, in hot oven 10 minutes. Reduce heat to moderate, bake further 30 minutes or until spatchcocks are browned and tender, brushing occasionally with marinade during cooking. Serve spatchcocks with glazed garlic peppers.

Glazed Garlic Peppers: Peel garlic, halve large cloves. Combine garlic, butter, oil, vinegar and peppers in pan. Simmer, uncovered, 5 minutes; cover, simmer further 30 minutes or until peppers are soft, stir in honey.

Serves 8.

■ Spatchcocks can be prepared a day ahead. Peppers can be made 3 days ahead.
■ Storage: Covered, in refrigerator.
■ Freeze: Uncooked spatchcocks suitable.
■ Microwave: Peppers suitable.

MARINATED CHICKEN DRUMSTICKS

1 tablespoon grated lemon rind
½ cup lemon juice
½ cup olive oil
½ cup brandy
½ cup white vinegar
3 cloves garlic, crushed
½ cup brown sugar, firmly packed
½ teaspoon ground cloves
1 tablespoon turmeric
1 teaspoon ground cumin
1 teaspoon garam masala
12 chicken drumsticks
2 tomatoes, sliced

BASIL DRESSING
½ cup olive oil
1 tablespoon white vinegar
2 tablespoons chopped fresh basil

Combine rind, juice, oil, brandy, vinegar, garlic, sugar, cloves, turmeric, cumin and garam masala in large bowl, add chicken,

cover, refrigerate several hours or overnight, turning occasionally.

Drain chicken, discard marinade. Place chicken on wire rack in baking dish. Bake in moderately hot oven for about 30 minutes or until lightly browned and

tender. Serve drumsticks with sliced tomato and basil dressing.
Basil Dressing: Combine all ingredients in bowl; mix well.

Serves 6.

■ Chicken can be marinated a day ahead. Dressing can be made a day ahead.
■ Storage: Covered, in refrigerator.
■ Freeze: Chicken suitable.
■ Microwave: Not suitable.

ABOVE: Clockwise from top left: Marinated Chicken Drumsticks, Honeyed Spatchcocks with Glazed Garlic Peppers, Rice and Chicken Liver Patties.

Plates from Country Floors

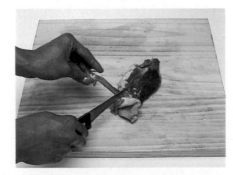

Trim end of wing bone.

Combine breasts, wine, brandy, vinegar, oil and bay leaves in bowl, cover; refrigerate several hours or overnight.

Remove breasts from marinade, discard marinade.

Heat extra oil in pan, add breasts, cook about 5 minutes each side or until browned and tender, remove from pan; keep warm. Heat butter in clean pan, add leek and bacon, cook, stirring, until leek is soft. Serve duck with leek mixture and red wine sauce.

Red Wine Sauce: Heat oil in pan, add onions, cook, stirring, 2 minutes. Add wine, water, stock cube, sugar, bay leaf, vinegar and jelly, bring to boil, simmer, uncovered, until onions are soft; remove onions from pan. Stir in blended cornflour and extra water, stir over heat until sauce boils and thickens. Remove from heat, stir in onions.

Serves 6.

- Duck can be prepared 2 days ahead. Sauce can be made 3 hours ahead.
- Storage: Covered, in refrigerator.
- Freeze: Not suitable.
- Microwave: Not suitable.

DUCK BREASTS WITH RED WINE SAUCE

3 double duck breasts
1 cup dry red wine
½ cup brandy
½ cup balsamic vinegar
1 cup olive oil
4 bay leaves
1 tablespoon olive oil, extra
60g butter
1 leek, sliced
4 bacon rashers, sliced

RED WINE SAUCE
1 tablespoon olive oil
24 baby onions
1 cup dry red wine
1 cup water
1 small chicken stock cube, crumbled
1½ tablespoons sugar
1 bay leaf
2 teaspoons white vinegar
2 tablespoons redcurrant jelly
1½ tablespoons cornflour
¼ cup water, extra

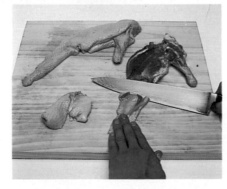

Remove excess skin and fat carefully from each breast.

Cut duck breasts in half.

Scrape meat down wing bone.

ABOVE: Duck Breasts with Red Wine Sauce.
ABOVE RIGHT: From top: Chicken with Fresh Fig Compote, Spicy Rabbit in Red Wine.

CHICKEN WITH FRESH FIG COMPOTE

½ cup water
½ cup castor sugar
2 tablespoons white vinegar
2 cloves
1 cinnamon stick
2 tablespoons port
1 lemon
1 tablespoon lemon juice
6 (about 500g) fresh figs
1½kg (about 12) chicken thigh cutlets
plain flour
¼ cup olive oil
1 tablespoon olive oil, extra
4 bacon rashers, sliced
½ cup dry white wine

Combine water, sugar, vinegar, cloves, cinnamon and port in pan. Cut rind from lemon using vegetable peeler, cut rind into long thin strips. Add rind and juice to vinegar mixture, bring to boil, remove from heat, add peeled and halved figs; cool figs in liquid. Strain figs, reserve ½ cup liquid; discard cloves and cinnamon.

Toss chicken in flour; shake away excess flour. Heat oil in pan, add chicken,

cook until browned but not cooked through; drain on absorbent paper.

Heat extra oil in clean pan, add bacon, cook until bacon is lightly browned. Add wine, bring to boil, simmer, uncovered, 2 minutes. Stir in reserved liquid from fig compote, bring to boil, simmer, uncovered, further 2 minutes.

Place chicken in single layer in large shallow ovenproof dish. Spoon bacon and sauce over chicken, cover, bake in moderate oven about 30 minutes or until chicken is tender.

Serves 6.

■ Chicken best made close to serving. Compote can be made 3 days ahead.
■ Freeze: Chicken suitable.
■ Microwave: Not suitable.

SPICY RABBIT IN RED WINE

1kg rabbit pieces
⅓ cup plain flour
2 teaspoons paprika
¼ cup olive oil
1 red Spanish onion, chopped
4 cloves garlic, crushed
2 dried chillies
2 bay leaves
½ teaspoon coriander seeds
½ cup dry red wine
¼ cup white vinegar
2 tablespoons tomato paste
2 small chicken stock cubes, crumbled
¾ cup water
1 tablespoon chopped fresh thyme
2 teaspoons sugar

Toss rabbit in combined flour and paprika, shake away excess flour. Heat oil in pan, add rabbit, cook until well browned all over; drain on absorbent paper. Transfer rabbit to ovenproof dish (8 cup capacity).

Add onion and garlic to same pan, cook, stirring, until onion is soft. Add chillies, bay leaves and seeds, cook, stirring, 1 minute. Add wine, vinegar, paste, stock cubes, water, thyme and sugar; bring to boil, simmer, uncovered, 5 minutes.

Pour mixture over rabbit, cover, bake in moderate oven about 2 hours or until rabbit is tender. Remove bay leaves and chillies before serving. Serve rabbit with buttered pasta twists, if desired.

Serves 6.

■ Recipe can be made a day ahead.
■ Storage: Covered, in refrigerator.
■ Freeze: Suitable.
■ Microwave: Not suitable.

ROAST QUAIL WITH APPLE BRANDY SAUCE

4 quail
15g butter, melted
1 tablespoon stale breadcrumbs

SEASONING
1 cup (70g) stale breadcrumbs
1 stick celery, chopped
2 cloves garlic, sliced
¼ teaspoon fennel seeds, crushed
2 tablespoons apple juice

APPLE BRANDY SAUCE
1 apple
½ cup apple juice
1 teaspoon cornflour
1 tablespoon Calvados
¼ cup water

Fill quail with seasoning, tuck wings under bodies. Brush quail with butter, sprinkle with breadcrumbs. Place quail on wire rack in baking dish. Bake, uncovered, in moderate oven about 40 minutes or until quail are tender. Serve quail with apple brandy sauce.

Seasoning: Combine all ingredients in bowl; mix well.

Apple Brandy Sauce: Peel and thinly slice apple. Combine apple and juice in pan, cook, covered, about 2 minutes or until apple is just tender. Stir in blended cornflour, brandy and water, stir over heat until mixture boils and thickens.

Serves 4.

- Quail can be prepared a day ahead.
- Storage: Covered, in refrigerator.
- Freeze: Not suitable.
- Microwave: Not suitable.

RABBIT CASSEROLE WITH OLIVES AND CAPERS

2 tablespoons olive oil
30g butter
800g rabbit pieces
2 onions, sliced
2 cloves garlic, crushed
410g can tomatoes
½ cup dry white wine
1 tablespoon chopped fresh rosemary
1 teaspoon chopped fresh thyme
1 bay leaf
1 tablespoon drained capers
16 black olives

Cut rabbit into 6 portions. Heat oil and butter in pan, add rabbit, cook until well browned all over; remove from pan. Discard all but 1 tablespoon pan drippings.

Add onions and garlic to pan, cook, stirring, until onions are soft. Stir in undrained crushed tomatoes, wine, herbs, bay leaf, capers and olives.

Place rabbit in deep ovenproof dish (6 cup capacity), add tomato mixture; cover, bake in moderate oven about 2 hours or until rabbit is tender. Remove and discard bay leaf.

Serves 4.

■ Recipe can be made a day ahead.
■ Storage: Covered, in refrigerator.
■ Freeze: Suitable.
■ Microwave: Not suitable.

CHICKEN AND HAM BALLS

300g chicken thigh fillets, chopped
½ cup dry white wine
½ cup water
2 small chicken stock cubes, crumbled
¼ cup orange juice
200g smoked ham, chopped
2 cloves garlic, crushed
1 tablespoon chopped fresh mint
40g butter
2 tablespoons olive oil
1 onion, finely chopped
⅔ cup plain flour
plain flour, extra
2 eggs, lightly beaten
⅔ cup packaged breadcrumbs, approximately
oil for deep-frying

Combine chicken, wine, water, stock cubes and juice in pan, bring to boil, simmer, uncovered, 10 minutes; cool, cover, refrigerate several hours or overnight.

Skim fat from stock, strain chicken from stock; reserve stock. Blend or process chicken, ham, garlic and chopped mint until almost smooth.

Heat butter and olive oil in pan, add onion, cook, stirring, until onion is soft. Stir in flour, cook, stirring, over heat until bubbling. Remove from heat, gradually stir in reserved stock, stir over heat until mixture boils and thickens; cool.

Combine sauce and chicken mixture, roll level tablespoons of mixture into balls.

Roll balls in extra flour, dip in eggs, toss in breadcrumbs. Place chicken and ham balls on tray; cover, refrigerate several hours or overnight.

Just before serving, deep-fry chicken and ham balls in hot oil until golden brown.

Makes about 35.

■ Recipe can be prepared a day ahead.
■ Storage: Covered, in refrigerator.
■ Freeze: Not suitable.
■ Microwave: Not suitable.

RABBIT, ARTICHOKE AND POTATO STEW

1kg rabbit pieces
plain flour
40g butter
1 onion, chopped
½ dry cup white wine
1 cup water
1 large chicken stock cube, crumbled
½ teaspoon dried thyme leaves
3 (about 350g) carrots
4 (about 500g) potatoes
275g jar artichoke hearts in oil, drained
2 tablespoons chopped fresh parsley

Toss rabbit in flour, shake away excess flour. Heat butter in pan, add rabbit, cook until well browned all over, drain on absorbent paper. Add onion to same pan, cook, stirring, until onion is soft.

Return rabbit to pan with wine, water, stock cube and thyme, bring to boil, simmer, covered, 20 minutes.

Cut carrots and potatoes into 1cm cubes, add to pan with artichokes and half the parsley. Simmer, covered, about 1 hour or until rabbit is tender.

Just before serving, sprinkle with remaining parsley.

Serves 4.

■ Recipe can be made 2 days ahead.
■ Storage: Covered, in refrigerator.
■ Freeze: Suitable.
■ Microwave: Not suitable.

LEFT: Clockwise from top: Rabbit Casserole with Olives and Capers, Chicken and Ham Balls, Roast Quail with Apple Brandy Sauce. ABOVE: Rabbit, Artichoke and Potato Stew.

SEAFOOD

These recipes are perfect for the natural way we like to eat seafood today. We've done casseroles fragrant with herbs, tomatoes, wine and olives, and lots of marinades to create special flavour magic in their particular dishes. Baking is easy and good; have you ever tried baked sardines? They're here to enjoy, as are roast salmon cutlets or baked fish with potatoes and crispy crumb topping. There's octopus, squid, and a generous seafood paella, great for casual times. For a dinner party, you could choose delicate salmon terrine, lightly fried lobster medallions in rich red wine sauce, and more.

SPICY MARINATED FISH

6 (about 1½kg) white fish fillets
oil for shallow-frying

MARINADE
½ cup chopped fresh coriander
4 cloves garlic, crushed
1 tablespoon paprika
pinch cayenne pepper
2 teaspoons ground cumin
¼ cup olive oil
2 tablespoons lemon juice
½ teaspoon cracked black
  peppercorns

Rub marinade into fish fillets, place in dish, cover, refrigerate several hours or overnight. Remove fish from marinade, discard marinade.
Just before serving, shallow-fry fish in hot oil until fish is tender.
Marinade: Combine all ingredients in bowl; mix well.

Serves 6.

■ Fish can be marinated a day ahead.
■ Freeze: Not suitable.
■ Microwave: Not suitable.

OCTOPUS WITH TOMATO SAUCE AND SPAGHETTI

1kg baby octopus
¼ cup olive oil
500g thin spaghetti

MARINADE
1 cup olive oil
1 cup dry white wine
3 teaspoons grated lime rind
¾ cup lime juice
2 cloves garlic, crushed
2 bay leaves
1 small fresh red chilli, sliced

TOMATO SAUCE
2 tablespoons olive oil
1 onion, finely chopped
1 stick celery, finely chopped
1 carrot, finely chopped
4 (about 1kg) tomatoes, peeled,
  seeded
⅓ cup tomato paste
1 tablespoon sugar

Remove and discard heads and beaks from octopus, cut octopus in half. Combine octopus and marinade in dish, cover, refrigerate 3 hours or overnight.

Remove octopus from marinade, discard marinade. Heat oil in heavy-based pan, add octopus, cook, stirring, in batches, until tender; keep warm.

Add spaghetti to large pan of boiling water, boil, uncovered, until pasta is just tender; drain. Serve octopus with pasta and tomato sauce.
Marinade: Combine all ingredients in bowl, mix well.
Tomato Sauce: Heat oil in pan, add onion, cook, stirring, until onion is soft. Add celery and carrot, cook, stirring, until vegetables are tender. Add chopped tomatoes, paste and sugar, stir over heat until boiling, simmer, uncovered, about 30 minutes or until slightly thickened.

Serves 4.

■ Octopus can be marinated a day ahead. Sauce can be made a day ahead.
■ Storage: Covered, in refrigerator.
■ Freeze: Not suitable.
■ Microwave: Pasta suitable.

FISH FILLETS WITH ORANGE PARSLEY SAUCE

4 (about 1kg) white fish fillets
plain flour
¼ cup olive oil
40g butter
1 red Spanish onion, finely chopped
1 tablespoon white vinegar
1 tablespoon drained capers
1 tablespoon grated orange rind
⅓ cup orange juice
80g butter, extra
1 tablespoon chopped fresh parsley

Toss fish in flour, shake away excess flour. Heat oil in pan, add fish, cook until tender. Remove from pan; keep warm.

Heat butter in clean pan, add onion, cook, stirring, until onion is soft. Add vinegar, capers, rind and juice, stir over heat until boiling, remove from heat; whisk in extra butter, stir in parsley. Serve orange parsley sauce with fish.

Serves 4.

■ Recipe is best made close to serving.
■ Freeze: Not suitable.
■ Microwave: Not suitable.

RIGHT: Clockwise from top left: Octopus with Tomato Sauce and Spaghetti, Spicy Marinated Fish, Fish Fillets with Orange Parsley Sauce.

GRILLED TUNA WITH SUN-DRIED TOMATO SAUCE

6 tuna steaks
¼ cup drained chopped sun-dried tomatoes
1 onion, chopped
4 cloves garlic, crushed
⅓ cup lemon juice
¼ cup olive oil
2 tablespoons balsamic vinegar
2 teaspoons sugar
1 teaspoon cracked black peppercorns
½ cup water
1½ tablespoons chopped fresh basil

Place tuna in dish. Combine tomatoes, onion, garlic, juice, oil, vinegar, sugar and peppercorns in bowl. Divide tomato mixture in half, reserve half to serve with tuna. Add water to remaining half of tomato mixture, pour mixture over tuna; cover, refrigerate several hours or overnight.

Drain tuna, reserve marinade.

Grill or barbecue tuna until tender, brushing with reserved marinade. Stir basil into reserved tomato mixture, serve at room temperature with tuna.

Serves 6.

■ Recipe can be prepared a day ahead.
■ Storage: Covered, in refrigerator.
■ Freeze: Not suitable.
■ Microwave: Not suitable.

BELOW: Clockwise from top left: Seafood and Tomato Casserole, Grilled Tuna with Sun-dried Tomato Sauce, Smoked Cod and Tomato Tart.
RIGHT: Salmon Cutlets with Tomatoes and Olives.

Below: Plates from Country Floors

SEAFOOD AND TOMATO CASSEROLE

2 medium leeks
⅓ cup olive oil
2 cloves garlic, crushed
2 sticks celery, chopped
2 x 410g cans tomatoes
2 bay leaves
pinch ground saffron
¼ cup dry white wine
2 tablespoons tomato paste
500g mullet fillets
500g snapper fillets
2 medium uncooked lobster tails
500g uncooked king prawns

GARLIC CROUTONS
½ cup olive oil
2 cloves garlic, crushed
1 small French bread stick, thinly sliced

Cut leeks into 3cm pieces. Heat oil in large pan, add leeks, garlic and celery, cook, stirring, until leeks are soft. Add undrained crushed tomatoes, bay leaves, saffron, wine and paste. Bring to boil, simmer, uncovered, about 15 minutes or until thickened slightly.

Remove skin from fish, cut fish into large pieces. Cut lobster, with shell intact, into rounds. Place fish, lobster and unshelled prawns on tomato mixture, simmer, covered, about 5 minutes or until prawns are cooked through. Serve with garlic croutons.

Garlic Croutons: Combine oil and garlic in bowl, brush both sides of bread with oil mixture. Place on oven tray, toast in moderate oven about 10 minutes.

Serves 6.

■ Recipe is best made just before serving.
■ Freeze: Not suitable.
■ Microwave: Not suitable.

SMOKED COD AND TOMATO TART

500g smoked cod fillets
1 cup milk
1 cup water
2 bay leaves
1 teaspoon black peppercorns
16 black olives, halved
1 tablespoon chopped fresh parsley

PASTRY
½ cup plain flour
1 cup wholemeal self-raising flour
180g butter, chopped
2 egg yolks
2 tablespoons water, approximately

TOMATO FILLING
¼ cup olive oil
4 green shallots, chopped
2 cloves garlic, crushed
4 large (about 1kg) tomatoes, peeled, seeded
1 tablespoon chopped fresh basil

Combine cod, milk, water, bay leaves and peppercorns in pan, cook gently without boiling, uncovered, about 10 minutes or until cod is tender. Drain cod, discard milk mixture. Remove skin from cod, break cod into large pieces.

Just before serving, gently stir cod, olives and parsley into tomato filling, spoon filling into pastry case.

Pastry: Sift flours into bowl, rub in butter. Stir in egg yolks and enough water to make ingredients cling together to form a firm dough. Press dough into ball, knead gently on lightly floured surface until smooth, cover, refrigerate 30 minutes.

Roll dough between sheets of greaseproof paper, until large enough to line greased 24cm flan tin. Lift pastry into tin, gently ease into side, trim edge.

Place tin on oven tray; line pastry with paper, fill with dried beans or rice. Bake in moderately hot oven 10 minutes, remove paper and beans, bake further 15 minutes or until well browned.

Tomato Filling: Heat oil in pan, add shallots and garlic, cook, stirring, 1 minute. Add chopped tomatoes and basil, cook, stirring, 5 minutes.

Serves 4.

■ Cod and tomato filling can be made a day ahead.
■ Storage: Separately, covered, in refrigerator.
■ Freeze: Not suitable.
■ Microwave: Cod and tomato filling suitable.

SALMON CUTLETS WITH TOMATOES AND OLIVES

½ cup raisins
4 salmon cutlets
plain flour
oil for shallow-frying
1 tablespoon olive oil
1 onion, chopped
1 stick celery, chopped
2 cloves garlic, crushed
2 x 410g cans tomatoes
1 cup water
2 bay leaves
150g pimiento-stuffed green olives
½ cup pine nuts, toasted

Cover raisins with hot water in bowl, stand about 15 minutes or until softened; drain.

Toss salmon in flour, shake away excess flour. Shallow-fry salmon in hot oil until lightly browned but not cooked through; remove from pan.

Heat olive oil in separate pan, add onion, celery and garlic, cook, stirring, until onion is soft. Stir in raisins, undrained crushed tomatoes, water, bay leaves, olives and nuts. Stir over heat until boiling, add salmon, simmer, covered, about 15 minutes or until salmon is tender.

Serves 4.

■ Recipe is best made close to serving.
■ Freeze: Not suitable.
■ Microwave: Not suitable.

ROAST SALMON CUTLETS WITH VEGETABLES

4 bacon rashers
2 tablespoons olive oil
2 onions, chopped
4 (about 500g) carrots, chopped
2 sticks celery, chopped
2 teaspoons chopped fresh thyme
2 teaspoons chopped fresh rosemary
1 cup dry white wine
½ teaspoon cracked black peppercorns
½ cup water
6 salmon cutlets
60g butter, melted
1 tablespoon lemon juice
2 tablespoons chopped fresh parsley

Cut bacon into thin strips crossways. Place bacon in pan, cook, stirring, until crisp; drain on absorbent paper.

Reserve 1 tablespoon of bacon fat in pan. Add oil, onions, carrots and celery, cook, stirring, until onion is soft. Stir in bacon, herbs, wine and peppercorns, bring to boil, simmer, covered, until vegetables are just tender; stir in water.
Just before serving, place vegetable mixture in greased large ovenproof dish, top with salmon, brush salmon with butter. Cook, covered, in moderate oven, about 30 minutes or until salmon is tender. Remove salmon from dish. Strain vegetables, reserve ½ cup of liquid.

Serve vegetables topped with salmon, reserved liquid, juice and parsley.

Serves 6.

■ Vegetable mixture can be cooked a day ahead.
■ Storage: Covered, in refrigerator.
■ Freeze: Not suitable.
■ Microwave: Suitable.

LOBSTER IN RICH RED WINE SAUCE

3 uncooked lobster tails
sprig fresh parsley
sprig fresh thyme
1 bay leaf
1 cup dry red wine
2 cups water
cornflour
30g butter
2 tablespoons olive oil
pinch paprika

RICH RED WINE SAUCE
30g butter
1 tomato, peeled, seeded
3 cloves garlic, crushed
1 carrot, chopped
1 onion, chopped
1 leek, chopped
30g ham, chopped
1 tablespoon plain flour
1 tablespoon tomato paste
pinch cayenne pepper
1 teaspoon paprika

Remove flesh in 1 piece from each lobster tail; reserve shells. Cut flesh into 2cm slices. Combine reserved shells, herbs, wine and water in pan, bring to boil, simmer, uncovered, 30 minutes; skim surface, strain stock. Reserve stock for sauce, discard shells and herb mixture.
Just before serving, toss lobster in cornflour, shake away excess cornflour. Heat butter and oil in pan, add lobster, cook on both sides until lightly browned and tender. Serve lobster with rich red wine sauce, sprinkled with paprika.
Rich Red Wine Sauce: Heat butter in pan, add chopped tomato, garlic, remaining vegetables and ham, cook, stirring, until carrots are tender. Stir in flour, cook, stirring, 1 minute. Remove from heat, gradually stir in combined reserved stock, paste, cayenne and paprika. Stir over heat until mixture boils and thickens.

Serves 4.

■ Lobster best prepared close to serving. Sauce can be made a day ahead.
■ Storage: Sauce, covered, in refrigerator.
■ Freeze: Not suitable.
■ Microwave: Sauce suitable.

PAN-FRIED TUNA
WITH ANCHOVY CAPER SAUCE

1 red pepper
¼ cup olive oil
4 tuna steaks

ANCHOVY CAPER SAUCE
½ x 45g can anchovy fillets, drained
2 green shallots, chopped
2 tablespoons chopped fresh
   flat-leafed parsley
2 tablespoons drained capers
1 clove garlic, crushed
1 teaspoon sugar
1 tablespoon lemon juice
⅔ cup olive oil
2 egg yolks

Quarter pepper, remove seeds and membrane. Grill pepper, skin side up, until skin blisters and blackens. Peel skin, cut pepper into strips.

Heat oil in frying pan, add tuna, cook until just tender. Serve tuna with anchovy caper sauce and pepper strips.

Anchovy Caper Sauce: Blend anchovies, shallots, parsley, capers, garlic, sugar, juice and 2 tablespoons of the oil. Add egg yolks, blend until combined. With motor operating, add remaining oil in a thin stream, blend until thick.

Serves 4.

■ Peppers and sauce can be prepared 3 hours ahead.
■ Storage: Covered, at room temperature.
■ Freeze: Not suitable.
■ Microwave: Not suitable.

LEFT: Roast Salmon Cutlets with Vegetables.
ABOVE: From top: Pan-Fried Tuna with Anchovy Caper Sauce, Lobster in Rich Red Wine Sauce.

Left: Plate and glass from Saywell; cutlery from Made Where

SQUID WITH RICE, BASIL AND PINE NUTS

¼ cup olive oil
1 onion, chopped
1¼ cups rice
1 litre (4 cups) water
¼ cup pine nuts
1 cup fresh basil leaves, firmly packed
4 cloves garlic, crushed
1 cup (80g) grated fresh parmesan cheese
¼ cup olive oil, extra
4 medium squid hoods

TOMATO SAUCE
5 (about 1¼kg) tomatoes, peeled, seeded
1½ tablespoons chopped fresh parsley
3 teaspoons cornflour
¼ cup water

Heat oil in pan, add onion, cook, stirring, until onion is soft. Add rice and water, bring to boil, simmer, uncovered, about 15 minutes or until rice is just tender and water absorbed. Blend or process nuts, basil, garlic, cheese and extra oil until smooth, stir into rice mixture.

Fill squid hoods with rice mixture, secure openings with skewers. Place hoods into ovenproof dish, add tomato sauce, cover, bake in moderate oven about 45 minutes or until hoods are tender. Remove hoods from dish, stand 15 minutes. Cut hoods into rounds, serve with tomato sauce.

Tomato Sauce: Roughly chop tomatoes, combine in pan with parsley. Stir in blended cornflour and water, stir over heat until sauce boils and thickens.

Serves 4.

■ Squid best cooked just before serving. Sauce can be made a day ahead.
■ Storage: Sauce, covered, in refrigerator.
■ Freeze: Not suitable.
■ Microwave: Sauce suitable.

PRAWNS WITH FETA CHEESE

⅓ cup olive oil
6 green shallots, chopped
3 cloves garlic, crushed
410g can tomatoes
½ cup dry white wine
2 tablespoons chopped fresh parsley
2 tablespoons chopped fresh oregano
2kg uncooked medium prawns, shelled
200g feta cheese, crumbled

Heat oil in pan, add shallots and garlic, cook, stirring, until shallots are soft. Add undrained crushed tomatoes, wine and herbs. Bring to boil, simmer, uncovered, about 15 minutes or until thick. Add prawns, simmer, uncovered until prawns are almost tender, stirring occasionally.

Just before serving, divide prawn mixture between 6 ovenproof dishes (1½ cup capacity), sprinkle with cheese. Bake in moderately hot oven about 5 minutes or until cheese is just melted.

Serves 6.

■ Prawn mixture can be made a day ahead.
■ Storage: Covered, in refrigerator.
■ Freeze: Prawn mixture suitable.
■ Microwave: Suitable.

SPICED FISH BALLS IN TOMATO SAUCE

450g white fish fillets, chopped
¾ cup stale breadcrumbs
3 cloves garlic, crushed
½ teaspoon turmeric
1 tablespoon paprika
1 teaspoon ground cumin
1 tablespoon chopped fresh coriander
1 teaspoon grated fresh ginger
1 egg, lightly beaten

TOMATO SAUCE
1 tablespoon olive oil
1 onion, sliced
1 clove garlic, crushed
410g can tomatoes
2 tablespoons tomato puree
2 tablespoons chopped fresh parsley
1 tablespoon chopped fresh coriander
½ cup water

Blend or process fish until minced. Add breadcrumbs, garlic, turmeric, paprika, cumin, coriander, ginger and egg; process until combined. Roll 2 level teaspoons of mixture into a ball, place on tray; repeat with remaining mixture. Cover, refrigerate 2 hours.

Just before serving, add fish balls to simmering tomato sauce, simmer, covered, stirring occasionally, until fish balls are cooked through.

Tomato Sauce: Heat oil in pan, add onion and garlic, cook, stirring, until onion is soft. Stir in undrained crushed tomatoes, puree, herbs and water. Bring to boil, simmer, uncovered, about 5 minutes or until slightly thickened.

Serves 4 to 6.

■ Fish balls and sauce can be made separately a day a ahead.
■ Storage: Covered, separately, in refrigerator.
■ Freeze: Uncooked fish balls suitable.
■ Microwave: Suitable.

RIGHT: Clockwise from top left: Squid with Rice, Basil and Pine Nuts, Prawns with Feta Cheese, Spiced Fish Balls in Tomato Sauce.

Bowls from Country Floors

FISH ROLLS WITH DILL BUTTER

10 (2kg) mullet fillets
1 egg white
½ cup stale breadcrumbs
1 tablespoon cream
1 teaspoon lemon pepper
4 green shallots, chopped
1 clove garlic, crushed
2 teaspoons chopped fresh dill
¼ teaspoon cracked black
 peppercorns
1 litre (4 cups) water

DILL BUTTER
80g unsalted butter
2 teaspoons chopped fresh dill

Remove and discard skin from 2 fish fillets, chop, then blend or process these 2 fillets until smooth. Add egg white, breadcrumbs, cream, lemon pepper, shallots, garlic, dill and peppercorns to fish, process until combined.

Gently pound remaining fish fillets between sheets of plastic wrap until even in thickness. Place 1 fillet, skin side down, on lightly greased foil, spread quarter of fish mixture along fillet, leaving 1cm border down each long side. Top with 1 fillet, skin side up. Roll foil tightly around fillets to form a roll. Repeat with remaining fillets and fish mixture.

Just before serving, place prepared rolls in pan, cover with the water, bring to boil, simmer, uncovered, about 15 minutes or until cooked through. Serve sliced, topped with dill butter.

Dill Butter: Combine butter and dill in pan, heat until butter is melted.

Serves 8.

■ Rolls can be prepared 6 hours ahead. Dill butter best made just before serving.
■ Storage: Rolls, covered, in refrigerator.
■ Freeze: Not suitable.
■ Microwave: Not suitable.

POTATO FISH BAKE
WITH CRISPY CRUMB TOPPING

1 tablespoon olive oil
2 cloves garlic, crushed
6 large (about 1½kg) tomatoes,
 peeled, chopped
¼ cup dry red wine
½ teaspoon cracked black
 peppercorns
1 stick celery, chopped
50g butter
5 (about 375g) onions, sliced
3 (about 500g)potatoes, thinly sliced
4 large (1kg) white fish cutlets

CRISPY CRUMB TOPPING
30g butter
¾ cup stale breadcrumbs
2 teaspoons chopped fresh marjoram
2 teaspoons chopped fresh thyme
2 teaspoons chopped fresh parsley

Heat oil in pan, add garlic, tomatoes, wine, peppercorns and celery. Bring to boil, simmer, uncovered, about 10 minutes or until

OCTOPUS AND RED WINE STEW

1kg baby octopus
2 tablespoons olive oil
3 onions, sliced
1 teaspoon curry powder
410g can tomatoes
2 tablespoons tomato paste
1 cup dry red wine
1 tablespoon drained capers
10 black olives, halved
1 tablespoon chopped fresh mint

Remove and discard heads and beaks from octopus, cut octopus in half. Add octopus to large pan of boiling water, simmer, covered, about 3 minutes or until

tender. Drain octopus; reserve.

Heat oil in pan, add onions and curry powder, cook, stirring, until onions are soft. Add undrained crushed tomatoes, tomato paste and wine. Bring to boil, simmer, uncovered, about 10 minutes or until slightly thickened.

Just before serving, stir in reserved octopus, capers, olives and mint, cook until heated through.

Serves 4.

■ Recipe can be prepared a day ahead.
■ Storage: Covered, in refrigerator.
■ Freeze: Not suitable.
■ Microwave: Not suitable.

mixture is thick. Heat butter in another pan, add onions, cook slowly, covered, until onions are soft.

Just before serving, add potatoes to pan of boiling water, boil, uncovered, 5 minutes; drain. Line base of greased ovenproof dish (10 cup capacity) with potatoes, top with fish, then tomato mixture, then onion mixture, sprinkle with crumb topping. Bake in moderate oven about 45 minutes or until fish is tender.

Crispy Crumb Topping: Heat butter in pan, add breadcrumbs, stir until lightly browned, stir in herbs.

Serves 4.

- Tomato mixture, onion mixture and crumb topping can be made separately a day ahead.
- Storage: Separately, covered, in refrigerator.
- Freeze: Not suitable.
- Microwave: Not suitable.

LEFT: Octopus and Red Wine Stew.
BELOW: Potato Fish Bake with Crispy Crumb Topping, Fish Rolls with Dill Butter.

Left: Dish from Lifestyle Imports; cloth from Les Olivades

SEAFOOD SALAD WITH BALSAMIC VINAIGRETTE

250g squid
1kg mussels
250g uncooked medium prawns
1kg pipis
½ red pepper, sliced
½ yellow pepper, sliced
100g black olives, halved
1 tablespoon drained capers
¼ cup chopped fresh parsley
2 tablespoons chopped fresh chives

BALSAMIC VINAIGRETTE
¼ cup olive oil
1 tablespoon balsamic vinegar
1 teaspoon lemon pepper
1 tablespoon lemon juice

Gently pull head and tail away from body of each squid. Remove clear quill from inside each body. Cut tentacles from heads just below eyes; discard heads. Remove side flaps and skin from hoods. Wash hoods, tentacles and flaps.

Chop tentacles, cut hoods and flaps into 2cm squares; mark inside surface of squares in diamond pattern. Scrub mussels, remove beards.

Bring large pan of water to boil, add squid and prawns, simmer about 3 minutes or until prawns are pink; drain.

Add mussels and pipis to another pan with a small amount of water, bring to boil, boil, covered, about 5 minutes or until shells open; drain.

Shell prawns, leaving tails intact. Remove mussel and pipi meat from shells; discard shells.

Combine all seafood in large bowl, add peppers, olives, capers and herbs with balsamic vinaigrette; mix well.

Balsamic Vinaigrette: Combine all ingredients in jar; shake well.

Serves 4 to 6.

- Recipe can be made a day ahead.
- Storage: Covered, in refrigerator.
- Freeze: Not suitable.
- Microwave: Suitable.

SALMON TERRINE WITH MUSTARD AND DILL SAUCE

1 bunch (40 leaves) English spinach

SALMON MOUSSE
4 (1kg) salmon cutlets
500g white fish fillets
3 cups milk
½ cup water
1 teaspoon black peppercorns
3 bay leaves
1 tablespoon chopped fresh parsley
50g butter, chopped
1 teaspoon grated lemon rind
1 tablespoon lemon juice
1 tablespoon dry sherry
3 teaspoons gelatine
2 tablespoons water, extra

MUSTARD AND DILL SAUCE
100g packaged cream cheese
1 cup cream
1 teaspoon seeded mustard
1 teaspoon chopped fresh dill
3 teaspoons lemon juice
½ cup water

Grease 10cm x 25cm loaf dish. Boil, steam or microwave spinach until wilted, rinse under cold water; drain well. Line prepared dish with spinach, allowing leaves to overhang edges of dish.

Spread half the mousse into prepared dish, top with reserved chopped salmon and white fish. Spread with remaining mousse mixture; press down firmly. Fold in overhanging spinach, refrigerate several hours or overnight. Serve sliced terrine with mustard and dill sauce.

Salmon Mousse: Combine salmon and white fish, milk, water, peppercorns, bay leaves, parsley and butter in pan, cook gently, uncovered, about 10 minutes or until all fish is tender. Remove fish from pan; strain liquid, reserve 1 cup liquid.

Remove skin and bones from fish, chop fish, reserve 1 cup salmon and ½ cup white fish. Blend or process remaining fish with reserved liquid, rind, juice and sherry until smooth.

Sprinkle gelatine over extra water in cup, stand in small pan of simmering water, stir until gelatine is dissolved. Combine gelatine mixture with processed fish mixture, mix well.

Mustard and Dill Sauce: Blend or process cheese and cream until smooth. Transfer mixture to small bowl, stir in remaining ingredients.

Serves 4 to 6.

- Recipe can be made a day ahead.
- Storage: Covered, in refrigerator.
- Freeze: Not suitable.
- Microwave: Suitable.

SEAFOOD PAELLA

12 (about 500g) large green-lipped mussels
¼ cup olive oil
1 onion, finely chopped
2 cloves garlic, chopped
1 chicken breast fillet, sliced
1 red pepper, chopped
1 green pepper, chopped
3 (about 400g) tomatoes, seeded, chopped
1 teaspoon sugar
2 cups long-grain rice
3½ cups water
1 small chicken stock cube, crumbled
¼ teaspoon ground saffron
2 bay leaves
1 large fillet ocean trout, chopped
1 large white fish fillet, chopped
300g cooked prawns, shelled, chopped

Scrub mussels, remove beards. Heat oil in large pan, add onion and garlic, cook, stirring, until onion is soft. Add chicken and peppers, cook, stirring, 1 minute. Stir in tomatoes and sugar, bring to boil, simmer, uncovered, until almost all liquid is evaporated.

Stir in rice, water, stock cube, saffron and bay leaves, stir until boiling, simmer, covered, 10 minutes. Stir in mussels, top with fish, cover, simmer about 5 minutes or until fish is cooked. Gently stir fish and prawns through rice before serving.

Serves 6.

- Recipe is best made close to serving.
- Freeze: Not suitable.
- Microwave: Not suitable.

LEFT: From top: Seafood Salad with Balsamic Vinaigrette, Salmon Terrine with Mustard and Dill Sauce.
BELOW: Seafood Paella.

MARINATED SNAPPER CUTLETS WITH BUTTER SAUCE

4 snapper cutlets
1 cup dry white wine
4 cloves garlic, crushed
1 tablespoon chopped fresh rosemary
1 teaspoon ground black peppercorns
plain flour
2 tablespoons olive oil
125g butter, chopped

Place cutlets in single layer in large shallow dish, pour over combined wine, garlic, rosemary and peppercorns, cover, refrigerate several hours or overnight.
Just before serving, drain fish from marinade, reserve marinade. Toss fish in flour, shake away excess flour. Heat oil in pan, add fish, cook on both sides until browned and cooked through; remove from pan, keep warm.

Heat reserved marinade in clean pan, whisk in cold butter a few pieces at a time. Continue whisking and adding butter over low heat until all the butter is used. Serve butter sauce with fish.

Serves 4.

■ Fish can be marinated a day ahead.
■ Storage: Covered, in refrigerator.
■ Freeze: Not suitable.
■ Microwave: Not suitable.

SARDINES BAKED WITH LEEKS AND TOMATOES

1kg sardines
1 tablespoon olive oil
2 large leeks, sliced
3 (about 500g) tomatoes, peeled, sliced
¼ teaspoon celery salt
2 tablespoons chopped fresh basil
2 tablespoons lemon juice
2 tablespoons olive oil, extra
1 tablespoon balsamic vinegar
2 cloves garlic, crushed
½ teaspoon sugar

Remove heads and entrails from sardines, wash sardines under cold water.

Brush shallow ovenproof dish with the oil, spread leeks into dish, top with a single layer of sardines, then a layer of tomatoes. Sprinkle tomatoes with celery salt and basil. Pour over combined juice, extra oil, vinegar, garlic and sugar. Cover dish, bake in moderate oven 30 minutes, uncover, bake further 10 minutes.

Serves 4.

■ Recipe can be prepared 6 hours ahead.
■ Storage: Covered, in refrigerator.
■ Freeze: Not suitable.
■ Microwave: Not suitable.

SEAFOOD WITH PEPPERS

500g small squid hoods
500g uncooked king prawns
12 small mussels
500g white fish fillets
2 tablespoons olive oil
¼ cup olive oil, extra
2 onions, sliced
2 cloves garlic, crushed
1 green pepper, chopped
1 red pepper, chopped
1 yellow pepper, chopped
2 x 410g cans tomatoes
¼ cup flaked almonds, toasted
pinch ground saffron
1 bay leaf
¼ cup dry white wine
1 tablespoon plain flour
2 tablespoons water

Cut squid into rings. Shell prawns, leaving tails intact. Scrub mussels, remove beards. Cut fish into 2cm cubes. Heat oil in pan, add seafood, cook, stirring, about 5 minutes or until seafood is cooked through; remove from pan.

Heat extra oil in pan, add onions and garlic, cook, stirring, until onions are soft. Stir in peppers, cook 2 minutes, add undrained crushed tomatoes, almonds, saffron, bay leaf and wine. Stir over heat until boiling, simmer, uncovered, 10 minutes or until peppers are soft.

Stir in blended flour and water, cook, stirring, until mixture boils and thickens. Add seafood, stir over heat until just heated through.

Serves 6.

■ Recipe is best made close to serving.
■ Freeze: Not suitable.
■ Microwave: Not suitable.

RIGHT: Clockwise from left: Marinated Snapper Cutlets with Butter Sauce, Sardines Baked with Leeks and Tomatoes, Seafood with Peppers.

fish. Serve fish with mushroom sauce.

Mushroom Herb Sauce: Heat butter in pan, add onion and mushrooms, cook, stirring, until onion is soft. Add flour, cook, stirring, 1 minute. Remove from heat, gradually stir in reserved fish stock. Stir over heat until mixture boils and thickens. **Just before serving,** whisk egg yolks and juice in bowl until frothy. Gradually whisk ½ cup mushroom sauce into egg mixture. Pour mixture into remaining mushroom sauce, stir in herbs, stir over heat, without boiling, until sauce is heated through.

Serves 4.

■ Recipe best made close to serving.
■ Freeze: Not suitable.
■ Microwave: Not suitable.

BAKED CHILLI SNAPPER

1½kg snapper
2 red Spanish onions, finely chopped
2 small fresh red chillies, finely
   chopped
6 cloves garlic, crushed
1 cup white vinegar
2 cups water
2 tablespoons sugar
2 tablespoons chopped fresh
   coriander
3 green shallots, chopped

Make 2 or 3 slashes across each side of fish in the thickest part, place fish in large baking dish. Combine remaining ingredients in bowl, pour over fish. Bake fish, uncovered, in hot oven about 30 minutes or until tender.

Transfer fish to serving plate; keep warm. Strain onion mixture; reserve onions, reserve 1 cup of cooking liquid. Blend or process reserved onion mixture with reserved cooking liquid, reheat, serve sauce with fish.

Serves 4.

■ Recipe best made close to serving.
■ Freeze: Not suitable.
■ Microwave: Suitable.

POACHED TROUT WITH MUSHROOM SAUCE

1 onion, quartered
2 carrots, chopped
6 black peppercorns
1 bay leaf
½ teaspoon dried thyme leaves
¾ cup dry white wine
2½ cups water
4 rainbow trout

MUSHROOM SAUCE
40g butter
1 onion, finely chopped
150g baby mushrooms, finely sliced
1½ tablespoons plain flour
3 egg yolks
2 tablespoon lemon juice
2 teaspoons chopped fresh thyme
2 tablespoons chopped fresh chives

Combine onion, carrots, peppercorns, bay leaf, thyme, wine and water in pan. Bring to boil, simmer, uncovered, 15 minutes, drain; reserve and cool liquid, discard vegetable mixture.

Place fish in single layer in large pan, pour over reserved liquid. Bring to boil, simmer, uncovered, about 10 minutes or until fish are just tender, drain; reserve 2 cups stock for sauce. Remove skin from

GRILLED SNAPPER IN HONEY FENNEL MARINADE

4 small snapper
20g butter, melted
1 teaspoon cornflour
2 tablespoons water

HONEY FENNEL MARINADE
¼ cup olive oil
¼ cup white vinegar
½ cup dry white wine
1 clove garlic, crushed
¼ teaspoon fennel seeds
1 tablespoon honey
1 teaspoon seeded mustard
¼ cup drained chopped sun-dried tomatoes
1 tablespoon chopped fresh parsley

Remove fins along back of each fish; score both sides of fish at 3cm intervals. Place fish in shallow dish, pour over marinade, cover, refrigerate several hours or overnight, turning occasionally.

Remove fish from marinade, reserve marinade. Place fish on greased foil, brush with butter, grill or barbecue until fish are cooked through.

Blend cornflour and water in pan, stir in reserved marinade, stir over heat until mixture boils and thickens, serve with fish.
Honey Fennel Marinade: Combine all ingredients in bowl, mix well.

Serves 4.

■ Recipe can be prepared a day ahead.
■ Storage: Covered, in refrigerator.
■ Freeze: Not suitable.
■ Microwave: Suitable.

LEFT: Baked Chilli Snapper.
BELOW: From left: Grilled Snapper in Honey Fennel Marinade, Poached Trout with Mushroom Sauce.

Left: Dish and tiles from Country Floors

BEEF

It's fascinating to discover how different beef can taste! Here are thick and warming country-style casseroles, braised beef with the salty tang of anchovies, and a chunky beef and potato pie. For our versions of famous dishes, try moussaka with lots of spinach and crunchy pine nuts, or pastitso, delicious with baked mince, cheese and pasta. If you prefer beef by itself, there's a simply elegant way to serve it with sun-dried tomato mayonnaise. However, if you like something extra tasty, try our steak roll where pepperoni sausage adds pep to the unusual seasoning.

SPINACH MOUSSAKA

3 large (about 1½kg) eggplants, sliced
plain flour
½ cup olive oil
9 large spinach (silverbeet) leaves, chopped
1 cup (155g) pine nuts
¼ cup olive oil, extra
1 onion, finely chopped
1kg minced beef
½ cup dry white wine
2 (about 250g) tomatoes, peeled, seeded
⅓ cup tomato paste
2 tablespoons chopped fresh mint
3 egg whites, lightly beaten
1½ cups (about 120g) grated Romano cheese

WHITE SAUCE
125g butter
1 cup plain flour
4½ cups milk
pinch ground nutmeg
3 egg yolks

Toss eggplant in flour, shake away excess flour. Heat oil in pan, add eggplant, cook in batches until lightly browned on both sides; drain on absorbent paper.

Boil, steam or microwave spinach until just tender, drain well. Combine spinach and pine nuts in bowl.

Heat extra oil in pan, add onion, cook, stirring, until onion is soft. Add mince, cook, stirring, until well browned. Add wine, chopped tomatoes, paste and mint, bring to boil, simmer, uncovered, about 15 minutes or until most of the liquid is evaporated; remove from heat, cool.

Stir egg whites into mince mixture. Cover base of ovenproof dish (12 cup capacity) with a third of the eggplant, top with a third of the white sauce. Spread over half the mince mixture then half the spinach mixture.

Repeat with half the remaining eggplant, half the remaining white sauce, the remaining mince mixture and the remaining spinach mixture. Finish with remaining eggplant and remaining white sauce mixture. Sprinkle with cheese, bake in moderate oven about 40 minutes or until heated through and evenly browned.

White Sauce: Melt butter in pan, stir in flour, stir over heat until bubbling. Remove from heat, gradually stir in milk, stir over heat until sauce boils and thickens. Remove from heat, cool slightly, stir in nutmeg and egg yolks.

Serves 8.

■ Recipe can be made a day ahead.
■ Storage: Covered, in refrigerator.
■ Freeze: Not suitable.
■ Microwave: Not suitable.

BRAISED BEEF WITH ANCHOVIES

1¼kg piece rump steak
¼ cup olive oil
¼ cup dry white wine
¼ cup red wine vinegar
¼ cup brandy
1 bay leaf
6 black peppercorns
¼ teaspoon dried thyme leaves
2 cloves garlic, crushed
2 tablespoons drained capers
½ cup sliced dill pickles
4 drained anchovy fillets, chopped
2 tablespoons cornflour
¼ cup water

Cut steak into 4cm cubes. Combine steak, oil, wine, vinegar and brandy in bowl; cover, refrigerate overnight.

Transfer steak and marinade to large ovenproof dish, add bay leaf, peppercorns, thyme and garlic; cover, bake in moderate oven 2 hours. Stir in capers, pickles, anchovies and blended cornflour and water, cover, bake about 20 minutes or until mixture boils and thickens.

Serves 4.

■ Recipe can be made 2 days ahead.
■ Storage: Covered, in refrigerator.
■ Freeze: Suitable.
■ Microwave: Suitable.

BEEF WITH SUN-DRIED TOMATO MAYONNAISE

1kg piece beef eye fillet
½ cup dry red wine
¼ cup olive oil
2 bay leaves, crumbled
1 teaspoon cracked black peppercorns
2 cloves garlic, crushed
1 tablespoon olive oil, extra

MAYONNAISE
½ cup drained sun-dried tomatoes, chopped
½ cup stale white breadcrumbs
⅓ cup lemon juice
½ cup water
2 egg yolks
1 cup olive oil

Combine beef, wine, oil, bay leaves, peppercorns and garlic in bowl, cover; refrigerate several hours or overnight.

Drain beef, pat dry with absorbent paper; discard marinade. Heat extra oil in pan, add beef, cook over high heat until browned all over. Place beef on wire rack in baking dish, bake, uncovered in moderately hot oven about 30 minutes or until cooked as desired. Stand beef 10 minutes. Serve with mayonnaise.

Mayonnaise: Blend or process tomatoes, breadcrumbs, juice, water and egg yolks until smooth. Add oil gradually in a thin stream while motor is operating.

Serves 4.

■ Beef best cooked just before serving. Mayonnaise can be made 2 days ahead.
■ Storage: Mayonnaise, in refrigerator.
■ Freeze: Not suitable.
■ Microwave: Not suitable.

RIGHT: Clockwise from left: Spinach Moussaka, Braised Beef with Anchovies, Beef with Sun-Dried Tomato Mayonnaise.

Serving ware from Lifestyle Imports; sun dial and clay pots from The Parterre Garden

BEEF AND HARICOT BEAN CASSEROLE

1½ cups (300g) haricot beans
1kg chuck steak
2 tablespoons olive oil
2 onions, chopped
4 cloves garlic, crushed
2 x 410g cans tomatoes
1 litre (4 cups) water
2 small beef stock cubes, crumbled
1 teaspoon cracked black
  peppercorns
2 bay leaves
250g mettwurst, chopped
¼ cup chopped fresh parsley

Place beans in bowl, cover with water, stand overnight, drain.

Cut steak into 2cm cubes. Heat oil in pan, add steak, cook in batches until well browned all over; remove from pan. Add onions and garlic to same pan, cook, stir-ring, until onions are soft. Return steak to pan, add beans, undrained crushed tomatoes, water, stock cubes, pepper-corns and bay leaves. Bring to boil, sim-mer, covered, about 2 hours or until steak and beans are almost tender. Add sausage, simmer, uncovered, about 30 minutes or until steak and beans are tender; stir in parsley.

Serves 6.

■ Recipe can be made a day ahead.
■ Storage: Covered, in refrigerator.
■ Freeze: Suitable.
■ Microwave: Not suitable.

HEARTY BEEF AND POTATO PIE

1½ cups plain flour
60g butter
¼ cup water, approximately
2 sheets ready-rolled puff pastry
1 egg, lightly beaten

FILLING
1kg chuck steak
2 tablespoons olive oil
2 onions, sliced
1 clove garlic, crushed
2 tablespoons olive oil, extra
2 cups water
2 small beef stock cubes, crumbled
1 teaspoon cracked black
  peppercorns
410g can tomatoes
2 large (about 500g) potatoes

Sift flour into bowl, rub in butter. Add enough water to make ingredients cling together to make a firm dough. Press dough into a ball, knead gently on lightly floured surface until smooth, cover, refrigerate 30 minutes.

Roll dough large enough to line base and side of deep 24cm pie plate, trim edges. Place pie plate on oven tray, line

Cut potatoes into 1cm cubes, add to meat mixture, bring to boil, boil, uncovered, about 10 minutes or until potato is tender and liquid has thickened slightly; cool. Refrigerate 2 hours or overnight.

Serves 6.

■ Pastry and filling can be made a day ahead.
■ Storage: Covered, in refrigerator.
■ Freeze: Suitable.
■ Microwave: Not suitable.

BEEF ROLL WITH PEPPERONI

½ cup stale breadcrumbs
2 bacon rashers, chopped
2 hard-boiled eggs, chopped
2 tablespoons chopped fresh parsley
1 clove garlic, crushed
1 egg, lightly beaten
600g slice topside steak
1 stick pepperoni
¼ cup olive oil
1 teaspoon dried oregano leaves
1 onion, chopped
1 carrot, chopped
1 bay leaf
1 clove garlic, crushed, extra
½ cup water
1 small beef stock cube, crumbled
⅓ cup dry red wine

Combine crumbs, bacon, hard-boiled eggs, parsley, garlic and beaten egg in bowl, mix well. Pound steak with meat mallet until thin, spread with egg mixture, place pepperoni in centre of mixture. Roll steak to enclose pepperoni, tie roll with string at 3cm intervals.

Heat oil in large baking dish, add roll, oregano, onion, carrot, bay leaf and extra garlic, cook, turning, until roll is well browned all over. Stir in combined water, stock cube and wine. Cover dish, bake in moderate oven about 1 hour or until roll is tender. Stand roll 10 minutes, remove string. Serve roll sliced with vegetables and pan juices.

Serves 4 to 6.

■ Recipe can be made a day ahead.
■ Storage: Covered, in refrigerator.
■ Freeze: Not suitable.
■ Microwave: Not suitable.

LEFT: From left: Hearty Beef and Potato Pie, Beef and Haricot Bean Casserole.
BELOW: Beef Roll with Pepperoni.

Left: Copper dishes from Corso de Fiori; cloth from Les Olivades. Below: Plate from Corso de Fiori

pastry with paper, fill with dried beans or rice. Bake in moderately hot oven 10 minutes, remove paper and beans, bake further 10 minutes or until pastry is lightly browned; cool.

Spoon filling into pastry case. Cut puff pastry into 2cm strips, place strips across filling to form lattice, trim edges. Brush edge of pastry with egg, place remaining strips around edge of pie plate, press firmly to seal. Bake in moderately hot oven about 15 minutes or until pastry is browned and filling heated through.

Filling: Cut steak into 1cm cubes. Heat oil in pan, add onions and garlic, cook, stirring, until onions are soft; remove onion mixture from pan. Heat extra oil in pan, cook steak in batches until well browned.

Stir in onion mixture, water, stock cubes, peppercorns and undrained crushed tomatoes, bring to boil, simmer, covered, 1 hour or until steak is tender.

PASTITSO

300g large bucatini pasta
2 eggs, lightly beaten
1 cup (80g) grated kefalograviera
cheese
2 tablespoons stale breadcrumbs

MEAT SAUCE
2 tablespoons olive oil
2 onions, finely chopped
500g minced beef
410g can tomatoes
¼ cup tomato paste
1 cup water
2 small chicken stock cubes,
crumbled
½ teaspoon ground cinnamon
2 tablespoons chopped fresh parsley
2 egg whites, lightly beaten

TOPPING
80g butter
½ cup plain flour
3½ cups milk
2 egg yolks
2 cups (160g) grated kefalograviera
cheese

Add pasta to large pan of boiling water, boil, uncovered until just tender; drain, rinse under cold water, drain. Combine pasta, eggs and cheese in bowl; mix well.

Press pasta into lightly greased 24cm x 30cm ovenproof dish, spoon over meat sauce, smooth surface. Spoon over topping, sprinkle with crumbs. Bake, uncovered, in moderate oven about 45 minutes or until lightly browned. Stand 10 minutes before serving.

Meat Sauce: Heat oil in pan, add onions, cook, stirring, until soft. Add beef, cook, stirring, until well browned. Stir in undrained crushed tomatoes, paste, water, stock cubes and cinnamon, bring to boil, simmer, uncovered, about 30 minutes or until thickened; cool. Stir parsley and egg whites into mince mixture.

Topping: Melt butter in pan, stir in flour, stir over heat until bubbling. Remove from heat, gradually stir in milk, stir over heat until mixture boils and thickens. Remove from heat, stir in egg yolks and cheese, stir until cheese is melted.

Serves 8.

■ Recipe can be made a day ahead.
■ Storage: Covered, in refrigerator.
■ Freeze: Suitable.
■ Microwave: Not suitable.

MARINATED BEEF CASSEROLE

1½kg chuck steak
2 tablespoons olive oil
250g speck, chopped
2 onions, chopped
2 carrots, sliced
1½ cups water
2 small beef stock cubes, crumbled
200g baby mushrooms, halved
¼ cup plain flour
⅓ cup water, extra

MARINADE
4 cloves garlic, crushed
strip orange rind
2 bay leaves
2 cloves
1 teaspoon black peppercorns
1 teaspoon dried thyme leaves
2 tablespoons red wine vinegar
1 cup dry red wine

Cut steak into 2cm cubes, combine with marinade in shallow dish, cover; refrigerate several hours or overnight.

Drain steak from marinade, strain and reserve marinade. Heat oil in pan, cook steak in batches until steak is well browned. Add speck, onions and carrots, cook, stirring, until speck is browned.

Transfer steak and speck mixture to ovenproof dish (12 cup capacity). Add reserved marinade, water and stock cubes, cover dish tightly with foil, cover with lid. Bake in moderately slow oven about 2 hours or until steak is tender. Stir in mushrooms and blended flour and extra water, cover, bake further 20 minutes or until mixture boils and thickens.

Marinade: Combine all ingredients in jug; mix well.

Serves 6.

■ Recipe can be made 2 days ahead.
■ Storage: Covered, in refrigerator.
■ Freeze: Suitable.
■ Microwave: Not suitable.

LIVER AND BACON IN TOMATO AND WINE SAUCE

750g calves' liver
2 tablespoons olive oil
3 bacon rashers, sliced
2 onions, sliced
1 clove garlic, crushed
1 bay leaf
1 teaspoon chopped fresh thyme
1 tablespoon plain flour
1 cup dry red wine
¼ cup tomato puree
¾ cup water
½ teaspoon sugar

Cut liver into 2cm slices. Heat oil in pan, add liver, cook until lightly browned on all sides, remove from pan; reserve.

Add bacon, onions and garlic to same

pan, cook, stirring, until onion is soft. Add bay leaf, thyme and flour, cook, stirring, until bubbling. Gradually stir in combined wine, puree, water and sugar, stir over heat until mixture boils and thickens, simmer 2 minutes.

Just before serving, stir reserved liver into onion mixture, stir over heat until liver is just cooked through.

Serves 4.

- Recipe can be prepared 2 hours ahead.
- Storage: Covered, in refrigerator.
- Freeze: Not suitable.
- Microwave: Not suitable.

BEEF AND RICE BAKE

1 tablespoon olive oil
1 onion, chopped
1 bacon rasher, chopped
500g minced beef
410g can tomatoes
2 tablespoons tomato paste
3 cups water
2 large beef stock cubes, crumbled
1½ cups long-grain rice
4 eggs, lightly beaten
¼ cup grated fresh parmesan cheese
¼ cup chopped fresh parsley

Heat oil in pan, add onion and bacon, cook, stirring, until onion is soft. Add mince, cook, stirring, until browned. Add undrained crushed tomatoes, paste, water and stock cubes, remove from heat. Stir in rice, eggs, cheese and parsley.

Pour mixture into well-greased shallow ovenproof dish (8 cup capacity). Bake, uncovered, in moderately slow oven 30 minutes, stir well. Return to oven, bake uncovered, about 1¼ hours or until firm.

Serves 6.

- Recipe can be made a day ahead.
- Storage: Covered, in refrigerator.
- Freeze: Not suitable.
- Microwave: Not suitable.

LEFT: Pastitso.
ABOVE: Clockwise from left: Marinated Beef Casserole, Beef and Rice Bake, Liver and Bacon in Tomato and Wine Sauce.

PORK & VEAL

These excellent roasts will give you much pleasure with their uncomplicated but different flavours. To serve hot, there is pork with 3 peppers and eggplant, or herb-scented veal with oregano and garlic mayonnaise. To serve cold, veal with pistachio seasoning is dressed with pine-nutty pesto. Also hot, of course, are hearty casseroles including osso bucco with almonds, saffron and olives, or there is veal and mushroom sauce, fabulous with potato gnocchi. More casual are our cornmeal pastries with pork and olive filling, or piping hot traditional-style pizza with salami and lots of luscious melting cheese.

PORK FILLETS WITH HONEY AND ALMONDS

15g butter
1/3 cup slivered almonds
1/4 teaspoon ground cumin
2 teaspoons grated orange rind
1 clove garlic, crushed
1 1/2 teaspoons honey
2 x 300g pork fillets
plain flour
1 tablespoon olive oil
1 leek, chopped
1/2 cup dry sherry
1 small beef stock cube, crumbled
1 cup water
100g butter, chopped, extra
1 teaspoon cornflour
1 teaspoon water, extra

Heat butter in pan, add nuts, cumin, orange rind and garlic, cook, stirring until nuts are lightly browned. Remove from heat, stir in honey, cool.

Cut pocket lengthways, halfway into centre of each pork fillet, fill with nut mixture, secure with toothpicks. Toss pork in flour, shake away excess flour.

Heat oil in pan, add pork, cook until well browned all over. Add leek and sherry, bring to boil, simmer, uncovered, 1 minute. Stir in combined stock cube and water, bring to boil, simmer, covered, about 40 minutes or until pork is tender. Remove pork from pan; keep warm. Strain pan juices, return juices to clean pan.

Just before serving, whisk extra butter into pan juices over low heat, stir in blended cornflour and extra water, stir until sauce boils and thickens. Serve sliced pork with sauce.

Serves 4.

■ Pork can be prepared a day ahead.
■ Storage: Covered, in refrigerator.
■ Freeze: Uncooked filled pork suitable.
■ Microwave: Not suitable.

*LEFT: Pork Fillets with Honey and Almonds.
ABOVE RIGHT: Seasoned Cold Veal with Pesto.*

SEASONED COLD VEAL WITH PESTO

1kg piece veal breast

SEASONING
1 tablespoon olive oil
1 onion, chopped
1 clove garlic, crushed
250g pork and veal mince
¼ cup chopped fresh parsley
2 tablespoons shelled pistachio nuts
¼ cup grated fresh parmesan cheese
¾ cup stale breadcrumbs
2 tablespoons chopped fresh basil
1 teaspoon cracked black peppercorns
1 tablespoon marsala

PESTO
¼ cup pine nuts, toasted
¼ cup grated fresh parmesan cheese
1 cup basil leaves, firmly packed
2 cloves garlic, crushed
1¼ cups olive oil

Pound veal with meat mallet until same thickness all over. Place seasoning lengthways on veal; roll to enclose seasoning. Wrap veal tightly in double thickness of greased foil. Place veal in baking dish, bake, uncovered, in moderate oven about 1½ hours or until veal is tender.

Stand veal in foil 15 minutes, remove foil from veal, drain veal well. Re-roll veal tightly in clean sheet of greased foil,

refrigerate several hours or overnight. Serve cold veal with pesto.

Seasoning: Heat oil in pan, add onion and garlic, cook, stirring, until onion is soft; cool. Combine onion mixture with remaining ingredients in bowl.

Pesto: Blend or process nuts, cheese, basil, garlic and half the oil until smooth; gradually add remaining oil in thin stream while motor is operating; blend until mixture is well combined.

Serves 8.

- ■ Roll is best made a day ahead. Pesto can be made a day ahead.
- ■ Storage: Covered, in refrigerator.
- ■ Freeze: Roll suitable.
- ■ Microwave: Not suitable.

VEAL CASSEROLE WITH GREEN OLIVES

5 bacon rashers
800g diced veal
1 tablespoon olive oil
500g (about 16) baby onions
2 cloves garlic, crushed
¼ cup tomato paste
½ cup dry white wine
1 small chicken stock cube, crumbled
1½ cups water
1 tablespoon chopped fresh sage
**⅔ cup (28) pimiento-stuffed
  green olives**
200g baby mushrooms, halved
1 tablespoon cornflour
2 tablespoons water, extra

Cut bacon into 1cm strips, add to pan, cook, stirring, until bacon is crisp, spoon into ovenproof dish (8 cup capacity). Add veal to same pan, cook in batches until well browned, add to dish.

Heat oil in clean pan, add onions and garlic, cook, stirring, until onions are lightly browned. Add paste, wine, stock cube, water and sage, stir until boiling, add to dish. Bake, covered, in moderate oven 1 hour. Stir in olives and mushrooms, then blended cornflour and extra water; cover, bake 20 minutes or until veal is tender.

Serves 4.

■ Recipe can be made 2 days ahead.
■ Storage: Covered, in refrigerator.
■ Freeze: Not suitable.
■ Microwave: Suitable.

SALAMI AND MUSHROOM PIZZA

15g compressed yeast
½ teaspoon sugar
½ teaspoon plain flour
½ cup warm water
1½ cups plain flour, extra
2 tablespoons olive oil
1 cup (100g) grated mozzarella cheese
100g sliced Italian salami
50g baby mushrooms, sliced
10 black olives, halved
100g sliced mozzarella cheese

TOMATO SAUCE
410g can tomatoes
2 cloves garlic, crushed
1 tablespoon tomato paste
1 tablespoon chopped fresh pasley
1 tablespoon chopped fresh oregano
1 tablespoon chopped fresh basil

Cream yeast, sugar and the ½ teaspoon flour in small bowl, stir in water. Cover, stand in warm place about 10 minutes or until mixture is frothy.

Sift extra flour into large bowl, stir in yeast mixture and oil, mix to a soft dough.

Turn dough onto floured surface, knead about 5 minutes or until dough is smooth and elastic. Return dough to large greased bowl, cover, stand in warm place about 20 minutes or until dough is doubled in size.

Turn dough onto lightly floured surface, knead until smooth. Roll dough large enough to line oiled 35cm pizza pan or 24cm x 32cm pan. Spread dough with tomato sauce, sprinkle with grated mozzarella, top with salami, mushrooms, olives and sliced mozzarella. Bake in hot oven about 20 minutes or until pizza is crisp.

Tomato Sauce: Combine undrained crushed tomatoes, garlic and paste in pan. Bring to boil, simmer, uncovered, about 10 minutes or until slightly thickened; remove from heat, stir in herbs.

Serves 6.

■ Recipe is best made close to serving.
■ Freeze: Not suitable.
■ Microwave: Not suitable.

ABOVE: From left: Salami and Mushroom Pizza, Veal Casserole with Green Olives.
ABOVE RIGHT: From top: Osso Bucco, Potato Gnocchi with Veal Sauce.

OSSO BUCCO

1½kg veal shanks (osso bucco)
plain flour
¼ cup olive oil
2 onions, sliced
2 red peppers, sliced
410g can tomatoes
2 bay leaves
1 cup dry white wine
2 small chicken stock cubes,
    crumbled
1 cup water
pinch ground saffron
1 tablespoon chopped fresh thyme
¼ cup slivered almonds, toasted
2 cloves garlic, crushed
12 black olives

Toss veal in flour, shake away excess flour. Heat 2 tablespoons of the oil in pan, cook veal a few pieces at a time until well browned; drain on absorbent paper.

Heat remaining oil in pan, add onions and peppers, cook, stirring, until onions are soft. Stir in undrained crushed tomatoes, bay leaves, wine, stock cubes, water and saffron.

Return veal to pan, bring to boil, simmer, covered, about 1 hour or until veal is tender, stirring occasionally. Stir in thyme, nuts, garlic and olives, stir over heat until heated through.

Serves 6.

- ■ Recipe can be made 2 days ahead.
- ■ Storage: Covered, in refrigerator.
- ■ Freeze: Not suitable.
- ■ Microwave: Not suitable.

POTATO GNOCCHI WITH VEAL SAUCE

4 large (about 750g) old potatoes
1 egg, lightly beaten
1½ cups plain flour, approximately
½ cup grated fresh parmesan cheese

VEAL SAUCE
¼ cup olive oil
1kg stewing veal, chopped
1 onion, chopped
2 cloves garlic, crushed
2 bay leaves
2 cloves
2 tablespoons tomato paste
½ cup dry white wine
2 small chicken stock cubes,
    crumbled
3 cups water
125g baby mushrooms, sliced
2 tablespoons chopped fresh parsley
1 tablespoon chopped fresh oregano

Boil, steam or microwave potatoes until soft; drain. Push potatoes through sieve into large bowl. Stir in egg and enough flour to form a soft dough, knead on lightly floured surface until smooth. Shape ½ level teaspoons of mixture into balls. Place ball in palm of hand, press floured fork on top of dough to make indentations and to flatten slightly. Repeat with remaining balls.

Add gnocchi in batches to large pan of boiling water, simmer, uncovered, about 3 minutes or until gnocchi rise to surface; drain. Toss gnocchi in cheese, serve with veal sauce.

Veal Sauce: Heat 2 tablespoons of the oil in pan, cook veal in batches until well browned. Remove veal from pan.

Add remaining oil to pan, add onion and garlic, cook, stirring, until onion is soft. Add veal, bay leaves, cloves, paste, wine, stock cubes and water to pan. Bring to boil, simmer, covered, about 1 hour or until veal is tender. Stir in mushrooms and herbs, simmer, covered, further 10 minutes or until mushrooms are tender.

Serves 4.

- ■ Recipe can be made 2 days ahead.
- ■ Storage: Gnocchi, covered, on trays in refrigerator. Veal, covered, in refrigerator.
- ■ Freeze: Suitable.
- ■ Microwave: Gnocchi suitable.

ROAST VEAL WITH OREGANO GARLIC MAYONNAISE

Veal can be bought already rolled and enclosed in a net, if preferred.

1¼kg boneless veal shoulder

MARINADE
3 cloves garlic, crushed
⅔ cup lemon juice
¼ cup white wine vinegar
2 tablespoons chopped fresh oregano
1 tablespoon chopped fresh thyme
1½ teaspoons cracked black peppercorns
⅔ cup olive oil

OREGANO GARLIC MAYONNAISE
3 egg yolks
2 cloves garlic, crushed
1 teaspoon French mustard
2 teaspoons white vinegar
⅔ cup olive oil
1 tablespoon chopped fresh oregano

Roll veal, tie with string at 2cm intervals. Combine veal and marinade in bowl, cover; refrigerate overnight.

Drain veal from marinade, reserve marinade. Place veal on wire rack in baking dish, bake, uncovered, in moderately hot oven about 1½ hours or until tender; brush occasionally with reserved marinade. Stand veal 10 minutes; remove string. Serve veal with oregano garlic mayonnaise.

Marinade: Combine all ingredients in bowl, mix well.
Oregano Garlic Mayonnaise: Blend or process egg yolks, garlic, mustard and vinegar until smooth. Add oil gradually in thin stream while motor is operating, blend until mixture is thick. Add oregano, blend until combined.

Serves 6.
- ■ Veal can be prepared a day ahead. Mayonnaise can be made a day ahead.
- ■ Storage: Covered, in refrigerator.
- ■ Freeze: Not suitable.
- ■ Microwave: Not suitable.

ONIONS AND VEAL IN RED WINE SAUCE

½ cup olive oil
900g (about 30) baby onions
800g diced veal
plain flour
2 cloves garlic, crushed
2 bacon rashers, chopped
2 bay leaves
⅓ cup brown sugar
1 tablespoon red wine vinegar
⅓ cup tomato paste
1 cup dry red wine
2½ cups water
1 small beef stock cube, crumbled
1 cup (150g) hazelnuts

Heat oil in pan, add onions, cook, stirring, until onions are lightly browned; remove onions from pan.

Toss veal in flour, shake away excess flour. Add veal to same pan, cook, stirring, until veal is lightly browned. Add garlic, bacon and bay leaves, cook, stirring, 2 minutes. Stir in sugar, vinegar, paste, wine, water and stock cube.

Bring to boil, simmer, covered, about 1¼ hours or until veal is tender. Add reserved onions and nuts, simmer, covered, further 5 minutes or until onions are tender.

Serves 4.
- ■ Recipe can be made a day ahead.
- ■ Storage: Covered, in refrigerator.
- ■ Freeze: Suitable
- ■ Microwave: Not suitable.

PORK AND OLIVE PASTRIES WITH TOMATO SAUCE

500g pork fillets, chopped
2 tablespoons olive oil
1 onion, chopped
2 cloves garlic, crushed
¼ cup dry white wine
1 tablespoon lemon juice
1 cup water
1½ tablespoons plain flour
2 small chicken stock cubes, crumbled
10 pimiento-stuffed green olives, sliced
¼ cup chopped fresh parsley
1 egg, lightly beaten

CORNMEAL PASTRY
2 cups plain flour
¼ cup cornmeal
125g butter, chopped
⅓ cup water, approximately

TOMATO SAUCE
1 tablespoon olive oil
1 onion, chopped
1 clove garlic, crushed
410g can tomatoes
2 tablespoons tomato paste
½ cup water
1 bay leaf
1 small chicken stock cube, crumbled
½ teaspoon sugar

Process pork until well minced. Heat oil in pan, add onion and garlic, cook, stirring until onion is soft. Add pork, cook, stirring, until pork is well browned. Add wine, juice, blended water and flour and stock cubes. Stir until boiling, simmer, uncovered, 10 minutes, remove from heat, add olives and parsley; mix well, cool.

Divide pastry into 8 portions, roll each portion to 14cm square, trim edges. Divide pork filling between pastry squares, lightly brush edges of pastry with water. Fold pastry over filling to form triangles, press edges with fork to seal.

Place triangles on greased oven trays, brush with egg, bake in moderate oven about 30 minutes or until well browned. Serve triangles with tomato sauce.

Cornmeal Pastry: Process flour and cornmeal briefly to mix. Add butter, process until mixture resembles breadcrumbs. Add enough water to make ingredients cling together and form a firm dough. Knead dough on lightly floured surface until smooth; cover, refrigerate 30 minutes.

Tomato Sauce: Heat oil in pan, add onion and garlic, cook, stirring, until onion is soft. Add undrained crushed tomatoes, paste, water, bay leaf, stock cube and sugar. Bring to boil, simmer, uncovered, about 15 minutes or until thick. Discard bay leaf.

Serves 4.

■ Recipe can be made a day ahead.
■ Storage: Covered, in refrigerator.
■ Freeze: Not suitable.
■ Microwave: Not suitable.

ROAST PORK WITH THREE PEPPERS

2 onions
2 tablespoons olive oil
1kg piece pork neck
8 cloves garlic, peeled
1 large red pepper, chopped
1 large green pepper, chopped
1 large yellow pepper, chopped
1 large (about 500g) eggplant, chopped
1 tablespoon red wine vinegar

Cut onions into wedges. Heat oil in baking dish, add pork, cook over heat until well browned. Bake, uncovered, in moderate oven 30 minutes.

Add onions, garlic, peppers and eggplant to dish. Bake further 1 hour or until pork is cooked through and vegetables are just tender. Sprinkle pork and vegetables with vinegar. Serve pork with vegetables and pan juices.

Serves 4.

■ Recipe is best made close to serving.
■ Freeze: Not suitable.
■ Microwave: Not suitable.

LEFT: Roast Veal with Oregano Garlic Mayonnaise.
ABOVE: Clockwise from top left: Roast Pork with Three Peppers, Pork and Olive Pastries with Tomato Herb Sauce, Onions and Veal in Red Wine Sauce.

Above: Plates from Amy's Tableware

LAMB

One of the most popular meats, lamb is found everywhere with the aromatic flavourings and accompaniments that make it so enjoyable. For instance, we've roasted it with lemon, garlic and rosemary, and served it with spinach and potato bake; another roast is seasoned with bacon, herbs and mushrooms, and eaten with crispy potatoes. For a change, there are yummy little lamb and bacon pies, chops in parmesan crust with lemon and capers, and marinaded grilled chops with thyme butter. Very special, too, are the little noisettes in a cream and brandy sauce, and the ragout with feta cheese nestling under a fillo crust.

LAMB IN PARMESAN CRUST WITH LEMON AND CAPERS

4 lamb leg chops
plain flour
1 egg, lightly beaten
1/4 cup grated fresh parmesan cheese
3/4 cup packaged breadcrumbs
2 tablespoons olive oil
60g butter
1 tablespoon lemon juice
2 tablespoons drained capers

Toss chops in flour; shake away excess flour. Dip chops into egg, then combined cheese and crumbs; press on firmly. Heat oil in pan, add chops, cook until tender; drain on absorbent paper, keep warm. Heat butter in clean pan, stir in juice and capers, stir until heated through. Serve chops with lemon sauce.

Serves 4.

- Lamb can be prepared a day ahead.
- Storage: Covered, in refrigerator.
- Freeze: Not suitable.
- Microwave: Not suitable.

SEASONED LEG OF LAMB WITH CRISPY POTATOES

2 1/2 kg leg of lamb, boned
80g butter
2 cloves garlic, crushed
1/2 teaspoon dried thyme leaves
4 large (about 800g) potatoes, sliced

SEASONING
1 tablespoon olive oil
3 bacon rashers, chopped
1 onion, chopped
200g mushrooms, chopped
1/4 cup chopped fresh parsley
1/2 teaspoon fennel seeds
1/2 teaspoon dried thyme leaves
1/2 cup stale breadcrumbs

Pound lamb with mallet to an even thickness. Spread seasoning over lamb, roll lamb to enclose seasoning, secure with skewer, tie with string at 2cm intervals.

Heat butter in baking dish, add garlic, thyme and potatoes, stir well, remove from heat. Place lamb on top of potatoes, bake, uncovered, in moderately hot oven 30 minutes. Turn lamb and potatoes over in dish, bake, uncovered, further 1 hour or until lamb is tender.

Remove lamb from dish, stand 10 minutes before removing skewer and string. Increase oven temperature to very hot, bake potatoes, uncovered, further 5 minutes or until well browned and crisp. Serve lamb with potatoes.

Seasoning: Heat oil in pan, add bacon and onion, cook, stirring, until onion is soft. Add mushrooms, parsley, fennel and thyme, cook, stirring, 1 minute. Remove from heat, add breadcrumbs, stir until well combined; cool.

Serves 6.

- Recipe can be prepared 3 hours ahead.
- Storage: Covered, in refrigerator.
- Freeze: Uncooked meat suitable.
- Microwave: Seasoning suitable.

LAMB PATTIES WITH TOMATO AND MINT SALSA

1kg minced lamb
1 cup (70g) stale breadcrumbs
1 onion, chopped
2 cloves garlic, crushed
2 eggs, lightly beaten
¼ cup chopped fresh mint
1 teaspoon cracked black peppercorns
1 teaspoon grated lemon rind
oil for shallow-frying

TOMATO AND MINT SALSA
3 (about 350g) tomatoes, chopped
1 small onion, chopped
2 tablespoons chopped fresh mint

Combine lamb, breadcrumbs, onion, garlic, eggs, mint, peppercorns and rind in bowl; mix well. Divide mixture into 12 portions, roll each portion into a ball, flatten slightly. Shallow-fry patties in hot oil until browned and cooked through. Serve with tomato and mint salsa.

Tomato and Mint Salsa: Combine all ingredients in bowl; mix well.

Serves 4.

- Patties and salsa can be prepared a day ahead.
- Storage: Separately, covered, in refrigerator.
- Freeze: Patties suitable.
- Microwave: Not suitable.

LEFT: Lamb in Parmesan Crust with Lemon and Capers.
ABOVE: From left: Seasoned Leg of Lamb with Crispy Potatoes, Lamb Patties with Tomato and Mint Salsa.

LAMB RAGOUT WITH FILLO CRUST

1½kg leg of lamb, boned
⅓ cup olive oil
1 onion, chopped
5 cloves garlic, crushed
1 tablespoon plain flour
½ cup tomato paste
1 teaspoon garam masala
½ teaspoon ground cinnamon
410g can tomatoes
⅓ cup chopped fresh parsley
250g feta cheese, crumbled
6 sheets fillo pastry
80g butter, melted

MARINADE
1 cup dry red wine
¼ cup lime juice
1 tablespoon balsamic vinegar
½ cup brown sugar, firmly packed
2 teaspoons dried rosemary leaves
1 bay leaf

Cut lamb into 3cm cubes. Combine lamb and marinade in bowl, cover; refrigerate several hours or overnight.

Drain lamb from marinade; discard marinade. Heat oil in large pan, add onion and garlic, cook, stirring, until onion is soft, add lamb, cook, stirring until lightly browned. Stir in flour, paste, then garam masala, cinnamon and undrained crushed tomatoes, bring to boil, simmer, covered, 1 hour or until lamb is tender. Remove lid, simmer, uncovered, 10 minutes, stir in parsley; cool.

Divide lamb mixture between 4 ovenproof dishes (2 cup capacity), top with cheese.

Layer pastry sheets together, brushing each with butter. Cut 4 rounds from pastry large enough to cover tops of dishes and overhang edge by 1cm. Lightly brush rims of dishes with butter, cover with pastry rounds, press around rims firmly.

Place dishes on oven tray, bake in moderate oven 20 minutes or until pastry is lightly browned.

Marinade: Combine all ingredients in bowl; mix well.

Serves 4.

- Recipe can be made a day ahead.
- Storage: Covered, in refrigerator.
- Freeze: Cooked filling suitable.
- Microwave: Not suitable.

GRILLED LAMB WITH THYME AND BUTTER BEANS

12 lamb loin chops

MARINADE
¼ cup olive oil
1 teaspoon grated lemon rind
¼ cup lemon juice
1 tablespoon chopped fresh thyme
3 cloves garlic, crushed
½ teaspoon cracked black peppercorns

THYME BUTTER
125g butter, softened
1 teaspoon grated lemon rind
2 tablespoons chopped fresh thyme
1 tablespoon chopped fresh chives
½ teaspoon cracked black peppercorns

TOMATO SAUCE
1 tablespoon olive oil
1 onion, chopped
2 cloves garlic, crushed
410g can tomatoes
½ teaspoon sugar
310g can butter beans, drained, rinsed

Combine chops and marinade in bowl, cover; refrigerate overnight.

Remove chops from marinade, discard marinade. Grill chops until tender, top with butter, serve with sauce.

Marinade: Combine all ingredients in bowl, mix well.

Thyme Butter: Combine all ingredients in small bowl, mix well. Shape butter into a log, wrap in foil, refrigerate until firm.

Tomato Sauce: Heat oil in pan, add onion and garlic, cook, stirring, until onion is soft. Add undrained crushed tomatoes and sugar, bring to boil, simmer, uncovered, 5 minutes. Add beans, stir until hot.

Serves 6.

■ Recipe can be prepared a day ahead.
■ Storage: Covered, in refrigerator.
■ Freeze: Butter suitable.
■ Microwave: Tomato sauce suitable.

LAMB NOISETTES WITH RATATOUILLE

8 small lamb noisettes
1 tablespoon olive oil
4 cloves garlic, crushed
¼ cup sour cream
¼ cup cream
2 teaspoons brandy
½ small beef stock cube, crumbled
¼ cup water

RATATOUILLE
2 small tomatoes, peeled, seeded
1 small (about 250g) eggplant
coarse cooking salt
¼ cup olive oil
3 (about 250g) zucchini, chopped
1 onion, chopped
2 cloves garlic, crushed
½ red pepper, chopped
½ green pepper, chopped
1 tablespoon chopped fresh basil
1 tablespoon chopped fresh parsley

Secure noisettes with toothpicks. Heat oil in baking dish, add garlic and noisettes, cook until browned. Transfer dish to moderate oven, bake, uncovered, about 10 minutes or until noisettes are tender. Remove noisettes from dish; keep warm.

Add creams, brandy, stock cube and water to pan juices, bring to boil, simmer 1 minute; strain. Serve noisettes with ratatouille and cream sauce.

Ratatouille: Chop tomatoes. Cut eggplant into cubes, sprinkle with salt, stand 30 minutes, rinse under cold water; drain on absorbent paper.

Heat 2 tablespoons of the oil in pan, add eggplant and zucchini, cook, stirring, until lightly browned; remove from pan. Heat remaining oil in pan, add onion, garlic and peppers, cook, stirring, until onion is soft. Return eggplant and zucchini to pan, stir in tomatoes. Bring to boil, simmer, covered, about 8 minutes or until vegetables are soft. Stir in basil and parsley, simmer, uncovered, about 2 minutes or until slightly thickened.

Serves 4.

■ Ratatouille can be made a day ahead. Lamb best cooked just before serving.
■ Storage: Covered, in refrigerator.
■ Freeze: Not suitable.
■ Microwave: Not suitable.

LAMB AND SUN-DRIED TOMATO OMELETTE

2 lamb leg chops
¼ cup olive oil
2 large (about 400g) potatoes, sliced
1 red Spanish onion, finely chopped
2 cloves garlic crushed
½ cup drained sun-dried tomatoes, sliced
½ cup black olives, chopped
¼ cup chopped fresh parsley
6 eggs, lightly beaten
2 tablespoons olive oil, extra

Grill lamb until lightly browned and cooked through, cool; slice.

Heat oil in large pan, add potatoes, cook, stirring, over a low heat until cooked through. Transfer potatoes to bowl using a slotted spoon.

Reheat half the oil in pan, add onion and garlic, cook, stirring, until onion is soft. Add onion mixture to potato, gently mix in lamb, tomatoes, olives, parsley and eggs in bowl.

Heat remaining extra oil in large omelette pan, add egg mixture, cook about 2 minutes or until well browned under-neath. Place pan under griller, grill until top is set. Cut into wedges to serve.

Serves 4.

■ Best made just before serving.
■ Freeze: Not suitable.
■ Microwave: Not suitable.

LEFT: From left: Grilled Lamb with Thyme Butter and Beans, Lamb Ragout with Fillo Crust.

ABOVE: From top: Lamb and Sun-Dried Tomato Omelette, Lamb Noisettes with Ratatouille.

CRUSTY TOPPED LAMB WITH MUSHROOM SAUCE

2 x 1kg lamb loins, boned
1 teaspoon chopped fresh rosemary
3 cloves garlic, crushed
½ teaspoon cracked black
    peppercorns
6 slices double smoked ham
2 tablespoons olive oil
¼ cup grated fresh parmesan cheese
⅔ cup stale breadcrumbs
30g butter

MUSHROOM SAUCE
½ cup dry red wine
50g baby mushrooms, sliced
1½ cups water
1½ tablespoons plain flour
20g butter, softened

Open lamb loins out flat, rub inside of each loin with rosemary, garlic and peppercorns, top with ham.

Roll up lamb, secure with string at 2cm intervals; brush with oil.

Place rolled loins on rack in baking dish,

bake, uncovered, in moderately hot oven about 20 minutes or until browned. Reduce heat to moderate, bake further 20 minutes, uncovered, or until tender.

Stand lamb 10 minutes, remove string. Combine cheese, breadcrumbs and butter in bowl.

Just before serving, press breadcrumb mixture over each loin, bake, uncovered, in moderate oven about 10 minutes or until lightly browned and heated through. Remove loins from rack, strain and reserve ¼ cup of pan juices; stand lamb

74

10 minutes before slicing and serving with mushroom sauce.

Mushroom Sauce: Heat reserved pan juices in pan, add wine, stir until boiling and reduced by half. Add mushrooms, bring to the boil, simmer, covered, until just tender. Stir in water, bring to the boil, simmer, uncovered, 3 minutes, remove from heat, stir in blended flour and butter. Return to heat, stir until sauce boils and thickens slightly.

Serves 8.

- Recipe can be made a day ahead.
- Storage: Covered, in refrigerator.
- Freeze: Uncooked rolled loin suitable.
- Microwave: Not suitable.

LAMBS' KIDNEYS IN SHERRY SAUCE

1kg lambs' kidneys
½ teaspoon cracked black
**   peppercorns**
60g butter
1 tablespoon chopped fresh parsley

SHERRY SAUCE
1 tablespoon olive oil
1 onion, chopped
1 clove garlic, crushed
1 tablespoon plain flour
1 small beef stock cube, crumbled
¾ cup water
2 tablespoons tomato puree
pinch ground nutmeg
pinch ground allspice
⅔ cup dry sherry

Remove fat and membrane from kidneys, cut kidneys into 2cm cubes, sprinkle with pepper; cover, refrigerate 20 minutes.

Just before serving, heat butter in pan, add kidneys, cook, stirring, about 1 minute or until cooked through. Add sherry sauce to pan, stir until heated through. Serve sprinkled with parsley.

Sherry Sauce: Heat oil in pan, add onion and garlic, cook, stirring, until onion is soft. Stir in flour, cook, stirring, 1 minute. Add combined stock cube, water, puree, spices and sherry, stir over heat until sauce boils and thickens.

Serves 4.

- Recipe can be prepared 3 hours ahead.
- Storage: Covered, in refrigerator.
- Freeze: Not suitable.
- Microwave: Not suitable.

LAMB KOFTA WITH TABBOULEH AND YOGURT SAUCE

500g minced lamb
2 eggs, lightly beaten
1¼ cups (120g) stale breadcrumbs
2 onions, grated
2 tablespoons chopped fresh parsley
½ teaspoon ground cinnamon
1 teaspoon ground cumin
½ teaspoon chilli powder
2 teaspoons turmeric
1 teaspoon ground allspice

TABBOULEH
⅔ cup burghul
2 cups chopped fresh
**   flat-leafed parsley**
2 tablespoons chopped fresh mint
1 large tomato, seeded, chopped
2 yellow peppers, chopped
¼ cup olive oil
2 tablespoons lemon juice
2 cloves garlic, crushed

YOGURT SAUCE
½ cup plain yogurt
2 teaspoons lemon juice
2 tablespoons tahini paste
1 clove garlic, crushed
2 tablespoons water

Blend or process all ingredients until smooth and pasty. Shape ¼ cup of lamb mixture around a skewer; repeat with remaining mixture.

Just before serving, grill or barbecue kofta until cooked. Serve with tabbouleh and yogurt sauce.

Tabbouleh: Place burghul in bowl, cover with hot water, stand 30 minutes; drain, squeeze dry. Combine burghul with remaining ingredients in bowl, cover, refrigerate 2 hours, stirring occasionally.

Yogurt Sauce: Combine all ingredients in bowl; mix well.

Serves 4.

- Uncooked kofta can be prepared a day ahead. Tabbouleh can be made 2 hours ahead. Yogurt sauce can be made a day ahead.
- Storage: Covered, in refrigerator.
- Freeze: Uncooked kofta suitable.
- Microwave: Not suitable.

LEFT: From top: Lambs' Kidneys in Sherry Sauce, Crusty Topped Lamb with Mushroom Sauce.
ABOVE: Lamb Kofta with Tabbouleh and Yogurt Sauce.

Above: Plate from Butler and Co/Zuhause

ROAST LAMB WITH SPINACH AND POTATO BAKE

1½kg leg of lamb
4 cloves garlic, sliced
¼ cup lemon juice
½ cup olive oil
2 teaspoons dried rosemary leaves

SPINACH AND POTATO BAKE
8 spinach (silverbeet) leaves,
    chopped
300g feta cheese, crumbled
1 teaspoon ground nutmeg
2 tablespoons olive oil
2 large onions, sliced
4 large (about 800g) potatoes, sliced
2 cups water
2 large chicken stock cubes,
    crumbled

Cut small slits in lamb, insert garlic. Place lamb on wire rack in baking dish, pour over lemon juice and oil, sprinkle with rosemary. Bake, uncovered, in moderate oven about 1¾ hours or until cooked as desired. Serve lamb with spinach and potato bake.

Spinach and Potato Bake: Boil, steam or microwave spinach until wilted; drain well, cool. Combine spinach, cheese and nutmeg in small bowl.

Heat oil in ovenproof dish, add onions, cook, stirring, until soft; remove from heat. Sprinkle half the spinach mixture over onions, top with potatoes, then remaining spinach mixture. Pour over combined water and stock cubes. Bake, uncovered, in moderate oven about 1½ hours or until potatoes are tender.

Serves 8.

■ Recipe is best made close to serving.
■ Freeze: Not suitable.
■ Microwave: Not suitable.

MARINATED LAMB KEBABS

1½kg leg of lamb, boned
1 teaspoon dried oregano leaves

MARINADE
¾ cup olive oil
½ cup lemon juice
2 small chicken stock cubes,
    crumbled
2 teaspoons cracked black
    peppercorns
4 cloves garlic, crushed
2 tablespoons chopped fresh oregano

Cut lamb into 3cm cubes. Combine lamb and marinade in large bowl, cover; refrigerate several hours or overnight.

Just before serving, thread lamb onto skewers, grill until well browned and tender; brush with marinade occasionally. Sprinkle with oregano.

Marinade: Combine all ingredients in bowl; mix well.

Serves 4.

■ Recipe can be prepared a day ahead.
■ Storage: Covered, in refrigerator.
■ Freeze: Not suitable.
■ Microwave: Not suitable.

LAMB AND BACON PIES

1 egg, lightly beaten
3 sheets ready-rolled puff pastry

PASTRY
1½ cups plain flour
30g butter, chopped
1 tablespoon lemon juice
¼ cup water, approximately

FILLING
2¼kg shoulder of lamb, boned
2 tablespoons olive oil
3 bacon rashers, chopped
2 onions, chopped
1 clove garlic, crushed
2 teaspoons chopped fresh rosemary
1 bay leaf
¼ cup tomato paste
1 litre (4 cups) water
2 small beef stock cubes, crumbled
1 teaspoon cracked black
    peppercorns
¼ cup plain flour
¼ cup water, extra
2 teaspoons chopped fresh
    rosemary, extra
2 tablespoons chopped fresh parsley

Spoon filling into cooked pastry cases. Brush edges with egg, top with cut out ovals of puff pastry, press on firmly, cut around edges with knife. Decorate pies with pastry scraps, if desired, brush with egg. Bake pies in moderately hot oven about 30 minutes or until pastry is browned.

Pastry: Sift flour into bowl; rub in butter. Stir in juice and enough water to mix to a firm dough. Press dough into ball, knead on lightly floured surface until smooth, cover, refrigerate 30 minutes.

Divide pastry into 6 portions. Roll each portion on lightly floured surface large enough to line base and sides of 6 greased oval pie dishes (¾ cup capacity), trim edges.

Place dishes on oven tray, cover pastry with paper, fill with dried beans or rice. Bake in moderately hot oven 10 minutes, remove paper and beans, bake further 10 minutes or until lightly browned; cool.

Filling: Cut lamb into cubes. Heat oil in large pan, cook lamb in batches until well browned; remove from pan. Add bacon, onions and garlic to pan, cook, stirring, until onions are soft. Stir in lamb,

rosemary, bay leaf, paste, water, stock cubes and peppercorns. Bring to boil, simmer, covered, 50 minutes, remove cover, simmer further 10 minutes or until lamb is tender; discard bay leaf. Stir in blended flour and extra water, simmer until mixture boils and thickens. Stir in extra rosemary and parsley; cool.

Serves 6.

- ■ Pastry cases and filling can be made a day ahead.
- ■ Storage: Pastry cases, covered, at room temperature.
  Filling, covered, in refrigerator.
- ■ Freeze: Cooked pies suitable.
- ■ Microwave: Not suitable.

COUSCOUS TIMBALES WITH LAMB AND VEGETABLES

1¼kg shoulder of lamb, boned
2 tablespoons olive oil
2 red Spanish onions, quartered
2 cloves garlic, crushed
1 cinnamon stick
2 small fresh red chillies
2 small beef stock cubes, crumbled
2 cups water
1 teaspoon seasoned pepper
425g can garbanzos, rinsed, drained
2 carrots, sliced
2 zucchini, sliced
2 tomatoes, peeled, chopped

COUSCOUS TIMBALES
2 cups (300g) couscous
1½ cups boiling water
180g butter
2 cloves garlic, crushed
2 teaspoons cumin seeds
2 teaspoons ground coriander
pinch ground saffron

Cut lamb into 2cm cubes. Heat oil in large pan, add lamb in batches, cook, stirring, until well browned; remove lamb from pan. Add onions and garlic to pan, cook, stirring, until onions are soft. Return lamb to pan, stir in cinnamon, chillies, stock cubes, water and pepper. Bring to boil, simmer, covered, about 1 hour or until lamb is tender. Stir in garbanzos, carrots, zucchini and tomatoes, bring to boil, simmer, covered, further 10 minutes or until vegetables are just tender. Remove cinnamon stick and chillies; serve lamb with couscous timbales.

Couscous Timbales: Combine couscous and the boiling water in bowl, stand about 3 minutes or until all the water has been absorbed. Heat butter in pan, add garlic, cumin, coriander and saffron, cook, stirring, about 1 minute or until fragrant. Add couscous mixture, cook, stirring, about 2 minutes or until couscous is well mixed. Press couscous mixture firmly into 4 greased timbale moulds (1 cup capacity). Stand 2 minutes before turning out of moulds.

Serves 4.

- ■ Lamb mixture can be made a day ahead. Couscous best made just before serving.
- ■ Storage: Lamb, covered, in refrigerator.
- ■ Freeze: Lamb suitable.
- ■ Microwave: Couscous suitable.

LEFT: Roast Lamb with Spinach and Potato Bake.
ABOVE: Clockwise from top: Couscous Timbales with Lamb and Vegetables, Lamb and Bacon Pies, Marinated Lamb Kebabs.

VEGETARIAN

Meals or entrees without meat are eaten often in Mediterranean cuisines, with pasta, couscous, vegetables, peas, beans and lentils served in countless satisfying ways. Pasta is very tasty here with broccoli and sun-dried tomatoes, and couscous is lovely with spiced golden pumpkin and sultanas in creamy saffron sauce. You'll also enjoy piping hot pumpkin and tomato stew, or mushroom and eggplant ragout. Colourful salads include one with artichokes, olives and sun-dried tomatoes, or artichokes with cheesy polenta. And, if cheese pleases you, we've used it lavishly in tasty crepes with pine nuts and basil.

THREE CHEESE CREPES WITH TOMATO SAUCE

⅓ cup grated romano cheese

CREPES
2 eggs, lightly beaten
¾ cup water
1 cup plain flour

FILLING
200g mozzarella cheese, finely
    chopped
1¼ cups (250g) ricotta cheese
¾ cup grated romano cheese
2 eggs, lightly beaten
2 tablespoons chopped fresh parsley

TOMATO SAUCE
2 tablespoons olive oil
1 onion, chopped
2 cloves garlic, crushed
2 x 410g cans tomatoes
1 teaspoon cracked black
    peppercorns
½ teaspoon sugar
⅓ cup pine nuts, toasted
⅓ cup shredded fresh basil

Divide filling into 8 portions, place a portion along centre of each crepe. Roll crepes to enclose filling. Place crepes seam side down in large shallow greased ovenproof dish. Pour over tomato sauce;

sprinkle with cheese. Bake, uncovered, in moderate oven about 45 minutes or until filling is set.

Crepes: Blend or process eggs, water and flour until smooth. Cover, stand 30 minutes. Pour 2 tablespoons of batter into heated greased heavy-based crepe pan, cook crepe until set and lightly browned underneath. Turn crepe, cook until lightly browned. Repeat with remaining batter. You will need 8 crepes for this recipe.

Filling: Combine all ingredients in bowl, mix well.

Tomato Sauce: Heat oil in pan, add onion and garlic, cook, stirring, until onion is soft. Stir in undrained crushed tomatoes, pep-

per and sugar; bring to boil, simmer, uncovered, about 5 minutes or until sauce is thickened. Stir in nuts and basil.

Serves 4.

■ Recipe can be made a day ahead.
■ Storage: Crepes: Covered with plastic wrap. Tomato sauce: Covered, in refrigerator. Filling: Covered, in refrigerator.
■ Freeze: Crepes suitable.
■ Microwave: Not suitable.

LEFT: Three Cheese Crepes with Tomato Sauce.
ABOVE: Vegetable Pots with Pastry Lids.

Above: Copper pot from Corso de Fiori; napkin from Les Olivades

VEGETABLE POTS WITH PASTRY LIDS

1 medium bunch (12 spears) fresh asparagus, chopped
30g butter
2 medium leeks, sliced
2 cloves garlic, crushed
200g baby mushrooms, halved
1 small chicken stock cube, crumbled
2 cups water
¼ cup dry red wine
1 tablespoon arrowroot
1 tablespoon water, extra
1 teaspoon lemon juice
1 tablespoon canned drained green peppercorns
1 sheet ready-rolled puff pastry
1 egg yolk

Lightly grease 4 ovenproof dishes (1 cup capacity). Boil, steam or microwave asparagus until just tender. Heat butter in pan, add leeks and garlic, cook, stirring, until leeks are soft. Stir in mushrooms, cook, covered, 5 minutes; stir in asparagus.

Combine stock cube, water and wine in pan, bring to boil, boil, uncovered, until reduced by half. Stir in blended arrowroot and extra water, juice and peppercorns, stir until mixture boils and thickens.

Combine sauce and vegetable mixture, spoon mixture into prepared dishes.

Cut pastry into rounds large enough to fit tops of dishes. Place pastry over vegetable mixture, brush with egg yolk, decorate with pastry trimmings, if desired.

Bake in hot oven about 10 minutes or until lightly browned and heated through.

Serves 4.

■ Recipe can be made a day ahead.
■ Storage: Covered, in refrigerator.
■ Freeze: Not suitable.
■ Microwave: Not suitable.

VEGETABLE COUSCOUS WITH SAFFRON SAUCE

1 (about 500g) golden nugget
    pumpkin
1 cup (150g) couscous
1 cup boiling water
125g butter
1 onion, finely chopped
1 teaspoon ground cinnamon
2 teaspoons curry powder
½ teaspoon ground nutmeg
½ cup sultanas
2 tablespoons olive oil
40g butter, extra
2 teaspoons paprika
4 hard-boiled eggs, chopped
1 small red pepper, sliced
1 mignonette lettuce

SAFFRON SAUCE
2 tablespoons dry white wine
2 x 10g sachets saffron strands
40g butter
150g punnet oyster
    mushrooms, sliced
300ml carton cream

DRESSING
¼ cup cider vinegar
½ cup olive oil
1 teaspoon sugar

Cut pumpkin into quarters, remove seeds, cut each quarter into 4 pieces. Boil, steam or microwave until tender; drain.

Combine couscous and boiling water in bowl, stand about 3 minutes or until all water is absorbed.

Heat butter in large pan, add onion, cook, stirring, until onion is soft. Add couscous, cinnamon, curry powder, nutmeg and sultanas, cook, stirring, until heated through; keep warm.

Just before serving, heat oil and extra butter in large pan, add pumpkin and paprika, cook until heated through. Serve pumpkin topped with saffron sauce, couscous mixture, hard-boiled eggs, pepper, torn lettuce leaves and dressing.

Saffron Sauce: Combine wine and saffron in small bowl, stand 10 minutes. Heat butter in pan, add mushrooms, cook, stirring, until mushrooms are just tender. Stir in undrained saffron mixture and cream. Bring to boil, simmer, uncovered, until slightly thickened.

Dressing: Combine all ingredients in jar; shake well.

Serves 4.

■ Recipe best made close to serving.
■ Freeze: Not suitable.
■ Microwave: Not suitable.

ARTICHOKE AND POLENTA SALAD

1 litre (4 cups) water
1 vegetable stock cube, crumbled
1 cup (200g) polenta
2 cups (160g) grated fresh
    parmesan cheese
1 medium (about 300g) eggplant
coarse cooking salt
¼ cup olive oil
1 clove garlic, crushed
2 (about 200g) zucchini, sliced
150g baby mushrooms, sliced
½ cup drained sun-dried
    tomatoes, sliced
½ cup black olives
540g bottle artichoke hearts, drained,
    halved
1 tablespoon balsamic vinegar
2 tablespoons olive oil, extra
¼ cup shredded fresh basil

Lightly grease 25cm x 30cm Swiss roll pan. Combine water and stock cube in saucepan, bring to boil, gradually add polenta, simmer, about 10 minutes or until thick, stirring occasionally. Remove pan from heat, add cheese; mix well. Spread mixture into prepared pan; cool.

Cut eggplant into 1cm cubes, sprinkle with salt; stand 30 minutes, rinse under cold water; drain on absorbent paper.

Heat oil in pan, add eggplant, garlic and zucchini, cook, stirring, 2 minutes, remove from pan; cool.

Combine eggplant mixture, mushrooms, tomatoes, olives and artichokes in bowl, pour over combined vinegar and extra oil; mix well.

Just before serving, cut polenta into triangles, add to salad; sprinkle with basil.

Serves 4.

■ Recipe can be prepared several hours ahead.
■ Storage: Covered, in refrigerator.
■ Freeze: Not suitable.
■ Microwave: Polenta suitable.

RIGATONI WITH BROCCOLI AND SUN-DRIED TOMATOES

400g broccoli, chopped
60g butter
¼ cup olive oil
2 large onions, sliced
2 cloves garlic, crushed
½ cup drained sun-dried
  tomatoes, sliced
2 tablespoons chopped fresh basil
2 tablespoons pine nuts
400g rigatoni pasta

Boil, steam or microwave broccoli until just tender, drain; keep warm.

Heat butter and oil in pan, add onions and garlic, cook, stirring, until onions are soft. Add tomatoes, basil and nuts, cook, stirring, until heated through; keep warm.

Meanwhile, add pasta to large pan of boiling water, boil, uncovered, until just tender; drain.

Serve pasta topped with broccoli and tomato mixture.

Serves 4.

■ Recipe is best made close to serving.
■ Freeze: Not suitable.
■ Microwave: Not suitable.

LEFT: Vegetable Couscous with Saffron Sauce.
ABOVE: From left: Rigatoni with Broccoli and Sun-Dried Tomatoes, Artichoke and Polenta Salad.

MUSHROOM AND EGGPLANT RAGOUT

1 large (about 500g) eggplant
coarse cooking salt
¼ cup olive oil
2 cloves garlic, sliced
1 onion, sliced
1 teaspoon paprika
¼ teaspoon ground allspice
¼ teaspoon ground cumin
300g baby mushrooms
1 tablespoon Worcestershire sauce
1 tablespoon brown vinegar
2 tablespoons dry red wine
1 teaspoon chopped fresh thyme
¾ cup water
2 tablespoons chopped fresh parsley

Cut eggplant into cubes, sprinkle with salt; stand 30 minutes, rinse under cold water; drain on absorbent paper.

Heat oil in pan, add garlic, onion, paprika, allspice and cumin, cook, stirring, until onion is soft. Add eggplant, mushrooms, sauce, vinegar, wine, thyme and water. Bring to boil, simmer, covered, 10 minutes, remove lid, simmer, further 10 minutes or until liquid is reduced by half; stir in parsley.

Serves 4.

■ Recipe can be made 2 days ahead.
■ Storage: Covered, in refrigerator.
■ Freeze: Not suitable.
■ Microwave: Suitable.

POLENTA TART WITH ROASTED PEPPERS

1 litre (4 cups) water
2 vegetable stock cubes, crumbled
¾ cup polenta
100g butter, chopped
2 tablespoons chopped fresh parsley
2 large red peppers, sliced
2 large green peppers, sliced
2 large yellow peppers, sliced
½ cup olive oil
2 tablespoons brown sugar
2 cloves garlic, crushed

Grease 22cm flan tin. Combine water and stock cubes in pan, bring to boil, gradually add polenta, stirring constantly; stir in butter. Simmer about 15 minutes, stirring oc-

casionally, or until mixture has thickened, stir in parsley. Pour mixture into prepared tin; cool until firm.

Combine peppers, oil, sugar and garlic in baking dish; mix well. Bake in moderate oven 1 hour, stirring occasionally. Cut polenta into wedges, serve with peppers.

Serves 4.

- Recipe can be made a day ahead.
- Storage: Covered, in refrigerator.
- Freeze: Not suitable.
- Microwave: Polenta suitable.

PUMPKIN AND TOMATO STEW

¼ cup olive oil
2 cloves garlic, crushed
2 onions, chopped
4 large (about 750g) tomatoes, peeled, chopped
1 teaspoon dried marjoram leaves
½ cup water
1 vegetable stock cube, crumbled
1¼kg butternut pumpkin, chopped
440g can corn kernels, drained
310g can red kidney beans, drained, rinsed
1 cup (125g) frozen peas

Heat oil in pan, add garlic and onions, cook, stirring, until onions are soft. Add tomatoes, marjoram, water and stock cube, bring to boil, simmer, uncovered, 5 minutes. Add pumpkin to pan, cook, covered, about 20 minutes or until pumpkin is tender. Add corn, beans and peas to pan, cook further 5 minutes or until heated through.

Serves 4.

- Recipe can be made 2 days ahead.
- Storage: Covered, in refrigerator.
- Freeze: Not suitable.
- Microwave: Suitable.

SPINACH AND CHEESE FLAN

1 bunch (40 leaves) English spinach, chopped
20g butter
2 green shallots, chopped
1 clove garlic, crushed
1 tablespoon chopped fresh parsley
1 cup (75g) grated gruyere cheese
3 eggs, lightly beaten
½ cup milk
⅓ cup cream

PASTRY
¾ cup wholemeal plain flour
¾ cup white plain flour
125g butter
2 tablespoons water, approximately

Boil, steam or microwave spinach until wilted; drain well.

Heat butter in pan, add shallots and garlic, cook, stirring, until shallots are soft; cool. Combine shallot mixture, parsley, cheese, eggs, milk and cream in bowl; mix well. Place spinach in pastry case, pour over egg mixture, bake in moderate oven about 25 minutes or until filling is set and lightly browned.

Pastry: Grease shallow 23cm flan tin. Sift flours into bowl, rub in butter. Add enough water to make ingredients cling together to form a firm dough. Press dough into a ball, knead on floured surface until smooth; cover, refrigerate 30 minutes.

Roll dough between sheets of greaseproof paper until large enough to line prepared tin. Lift pastry into tin gently, ease into sides, trim edge. Place tin on oven tray, line pastry with paper, fill with dried beans or rice. Bake in moderate oven 10 minutes, remove paper and beans, bake further 10 minutes or until lightly browned; cool.

Serves 4.

- Recipe can be made a day ahead.
- Storage: Covered, in refrigerator.
- Freeze: Not suitable.
- Microwave: Not suitable.

LEFT: Mushroom and Eggplant Ragout, Polenta Tart with Roasted Peppers.
ABOVE: From top: Spinach and Cheese Flan, Pumpkin and Tomato Stew.

Left: Copperware from Corso de Fiori; tiles from Country Floors

ACCOMPANIMENTS

Rich and robust, the flavours of the Mediterranean surpass themselves in the many delightful ways they combine in these salads and accompaniments. Included in this section are hot and cold recipes: leafy green salads, fried cheese, old faithfuls like ratatouille and salad nicoise, and more recent favourites like olive and herb bread, and many more. Most have generous lashings of cheese and fresh, fragrant herbs. These versatile dishes can be served as main courses or entrees, and will be suitable either for a light luncheon, or a barbecue. We have also included step-by-step photographs on how to prepare fresh artichokes.

DEEP-FRIED CAULIFLOWER WITH CUCUMBER DIP

1 small (about 500g) cauliflower, chopped
plain flour
oil for deep-frying

BATTER
1 cup plain flour
1 teaspoon garam masala
1 teaspoon turmeric
1¼ cups milk
3 eggs, lightly beaten

CUCUMBER DIP
1 long thin green cucumber, peeled
2 tablespoons coarse cooking salt
½ cup black olives, pitted
45g can anchovy fillets, drained
1½ tablespoons lime juice
2 tablespoons shredded fresh basil
1 small red pepper, finely chopped

Boil, steam or microwave cauliflower until just tender, drain, rinse under cold water; drain well.

Toss cauliflower in flour, shake away excess flour. Dip cauliflower in batter, deep-fry in hot oil until lightly browned; drain on absorbent paper. Serve cauliflower with cucumber dip.

Batter: Sift dry ingredients into bowl, gradually stir in combined milk and eggs, beat until smooth.

Cucumber Dip: Seed cucumber, slice thinly. Combine cucumber and salt in bowl stand 2 hours, rinse under cold water, pat dry on absorbent paper. Blend or process cucumber, olives, anchovies and juice until smooth, stir in basil and pepper.

Serves 6.
- Cauliflower best cooked close to serving. Dip can be made a day ahead.
- Storage: Dip, covered, in refrigerator.
- Freeze: Not suitable.
- Microwave: Cauliflower suitable.

ARTICHOKE SALAD WITH ORANGE DRESSING

1 large (about 500g) eggplant, chopped
2 tablespoons lemon juice
coarse cooking salt
1 red pepper, thinly sliced
1 green pepper, thinly sliced
200g can artichoke hearts, drained, halved
¼ cup olive oil

ORANGE DRESSING
2 teaspoons canned drained green peppercorns
4 oranges, segmented
2 tablespoons white vinegar
2 teaspoons grated lime rind
2 tablespoons lime juice
½ cup orange juice
2 teaspoons sugar
1 tablespoon brandy
1 cup olive oil

Combine eggplant and juice in bowl, sprinkle with salt, stand 1 hour.

Rinse eggplant under cold water; drain well, pat dry on absorbent paper.

Fry eggplant, peppers and artichokes separately in the oil, until lightly browned; drain well, cool.

Combine vegetables and orange dressing in bowl; cover, refrigerate several hours before serving.

Orange Dressing: Combine peppercorns, orange segments, vinegar, rind, juices, sugar and brandy in pan, bring to boil, boil, uncovered, about 5 minutes or until liquid is reduced by half, stir in oil.

Serves 6.
- Recipe can be made a day ahead.
- Storage: Covered, in refrigerator.
- Freeze: Not suitable.
- Microwave: Not suitable.

SNOW PEAS WITH ANCHOVIES AND PEPPERS

1 medium (about 300g) eggplant, chopped
1 tablespoon lemon juice
coarse cooking salt
150g snow peas
1 red pepper, chopped
1 green pepper, chopped
1 yellow pepper, chopped
4 dill pickles, sliced
1 cup black olives
1 tomato, chopped
45g can anchovy fillets, drained

DRESSING
½ cup white vinegar
½ cup olive oil
¼ cup water
1 teaspoon sugar
2 teaspoons dried tarragon leaves

Combine eggplant and juice in bowl, sprinkle with salt, stand 1 hour.

Rinse eggplant under cold water; drain, pat dry with absorbent paper. Boil, steam or microwave peas until just tender, cool under cold water; drain well.

Combine eggplant, peas, peppers, pickles, olives, tomato, anchovies and dressing in bowl, mix well.

Dressing: Combine all ingredients in jar; shake well.

Serves 8.
- Recipe can be prepared a day ahead.
- Storage: Covered, in refrigerator.
- Freeze: Not suitable.
- Microwave: Snow peas suitable.

RIGHT: Clockwise from left: Snow Peas with Anchovies and Peppers, Artichoke Salad with Orange Dressing, Deep-fried Cauliflower with Cucumber Dip.

SPICY BROAD BEAN SALAD

1½ litres (6 cups) water
2 small chicken stock cubes,
    crumbled
2 teaspoons dried chilli flakes
500g frozen broad beans
100g csabai salami, sliced
2 tablespoons chopped fresh parsley
⅓ cup lemon juice
2 tablespoons olive oil

Combine water, stock cubes and chilli flakes in pan, bring to boil. Add beans, simmer, covered, about 10 minutes or until beans are tender; drain well, cool.

Combined beans, salami and parsley in bowl, add combined juice and oil; mix well.

Serves 4.

■ Salad can be made a day ahead.
■ Storage: Covered, in refrigerator.
■ Freeze: Not suitable.
■ Microwave: Suitable.

ARTICHOKES WITH VEGETABLE AND HAM SEASONING

6 large fresh artichokes
1¼ cups dry white wine
1 cup water
1 small chicken stock cube, crumbled
2 tablespoons cream
20g butter, melted
1 tablespoon cornflour
1 tablespoon water, extra

VEGETABLE AND HAM SEASONING
15g butter
1 onion, chopped
1 clove garlic, crushed
250g mushrooms, chopped
1 tablespoon chopped fresh parsley
1 tablespoon chopped fresh chives
3 slices (60g) ham, chopped
400g pork fillet, minced
1 egg, lightly beaten
1 carrot, grated

Trim base of artichokes so they sit flat. Remove tough outer leaves and trim remaining leaves with scissors (see picture below).

Boil, steam or microwave artichokes until just tender, drain; cool. Pull away some inside leaves and coarse centre with spoon (see picture below).

Spoon filling into centre of each artichoke. Tie string around outer edge of each artichoke to hold leaves in shape.

Pour wine, water and stock cube into baking dish. Place artichokes in dish, cover, bake in moderate oven about 40 minutes or until filling is cooked.

Remove artichokes from dish; keep warm. Strain cooking liquid into pan, bring to boil, simmer, uncovered, 5 minutes. Stir in cream, butter, and blended cornflour and extra water, cook, stirring, until sauce boils and thickens. Serve with artichokes.

Vegetable and Ham Seasoning: Heat butter in pan, add onion and garlic, cook, stirring, until onion is soft. Stir in mushrooms, parsley and chives, cook, stirring, until mushrooms are just tender; cool. Combine mushroom mixture with remaining ingredients in bowl, mix well.

Serves 6.

- Recipe is best made close to serving.
- Freeze: Not suitable.
- Microwave: Artichokes suitable.

EGGPLANT MOULDS WITH YOGURT SAUCE

3 small (about 750g) eggplants
coarse cooking salt
¼ cup stale breadcrumbs

CHEESE FILLING
1 cup (200g) ricotta cheese
¾ cup grated tasty cheese
1 onion, chopped
50g mushrooms, chopped
1 small red pepper, chopped
3 eggs, lightly beaten
¼ cup stale breadcrumbs
1 tablespoon chopped fresh parsley
1 teaspoon chopped fresh dill
½ teaspoon cracked black
**   peppercorns**

YOGURT SAUCE
¼ cup sour cream
¼ cup yogurt
1 small green cucumber, seeded,
**   chopped**
1 small red pepper, chopped
1 tablespoon chopped fresh parsley

Cut eggplants into 5mm thick slices, sprinkle with salt, stand 30 minutes.

Rinse eggplant slices under cold water, pat dry with absorbent paper. Grill eggplant until lightly browned; cool. Lightly grease 6 ovenproof moulds (¾ cup capacity); sprinkle with breadcrumbs. Line moulds with eggplant slices, spread cheese filling into moulds. Place moulds onto oven tray, bake, covered, in moderate oven about 35 minutes or until set. Stand 5 minutes before turning onto plates. Serve hot with yogurt sauce.

Cheese Filling: Combine all ingredients in bowl; mix well.

Yogurt Sauce: Combine all ingredients in bowl; mix well.

Serves 6.

- Moulds and sauce can be made separately a day ahead.
- Storage: Covered, in refrigerator.
- Freeze: Not suitable.
- Microwave: Not suitable.

LEFT: From left: Spicy Broad Bean Salad, Artichokes with Vegetable and Ham Seasoning.
BELOW: Eggplant Moulds with Yogurt Sauce.

Left: Plates from Corso de Fiori

CAULIFLOWER SALAD WITH PARMESAN DRESSING

1 medium (about 800g) cauliflower, chopped
200g okra
3 red Spanish onions, finely chopped
1 red pepper, finely chopped

PARMESAN DRESSING
1 cup cider vinegar
1 cup water
1 cup (80g) grated fresh parmesan cheese
3 cloves garlic, crushed
3 teaspoons sugar
2 teaspoons dried oregano leaves

Boil, steam or microwave cauliflower and okra separately until just tender, drain; rinse under cold water, drain.

Combine cauliflower, okra, onions, pepper and parmesan dressing in bowl; refrigerate several hours or overnight.
Dressing: Combine all ingredients in bowl; mix well.

Serves 6.

■ Recipe can be made a day ahead.
■ Storage: Covered, in refrigerator.
■ Freeze: Not suitable.
■ Microwave: Vegetables suitable.

RICE MOULD WITH SPICY MAYONNAISE

1 tablespoon olive oil
1 cup short grain rice
1½ cups boiling water
2 small chicken stock cubes, crumbled
½ teaspoon chopped fresh thyme
½ teaspoon chopped fresh tarragon
1 red pepper, finely chopped
185g can tuna, drained
75g salami, chopped
2 tablespoons chopped fresh parsley

SPICY MAYONNAISE
2 egg yolks
1 tablespoon lemon juice
¾ cup olive oil
1 teaspoon Worcestershire sauce
2 tablespoons tomato sauce
dash tabasco sauce
1 teaspoon paprika

Heat oil in heavy-based pan, add rice, stir over heat 2 minutes. Add water and stock cubes, bring to boil, simmer, covered, about 12 minutes or until rice is tender and water absorbed. Transfer rice to bowl, cool. Stir in thyme, tarragon, pepper, tuna, salami and ½ cup of the spicy mayonnaise. Press mixture into lightly greased 22cm savarin pan, cover, refrigerate several hours or overnight.

Turn mould onto serving plate, sprinkle with parsley, drizzle with remaining spicy mayonnaise.

Spicy Mayonnaise: Blend or process egg yolks and juice until thick and pale. With blender operating, pour in oil in thin stream. Transfer mixture to bowl, stir in sauces and paprika.

Serves 8.

- Rice mould and mayonnaise can be made a day ahead.
- Storage: Covered, in refrigerator.
- Freeze: Not suitable.
- Microwave: Not suitable.

TOMATOES WITH NUTTY WILD RICE SEASONING

12 small tomatoes
2 tablespoons olive oil
1 onion, finely chopped
2 cloves garlic, crushed
250g minced beef
1 teaspoon turmeric
1 teaspoon garam masala
2 teaspoons sugar
½ teaspoon grated lime rind
2 tablespoons lime juice
¼ cup pine nuts
¾ cup cooked rice
¼ cup cooked wild rice
¼ cup dried apples, finely chopped
¼ teaspoon ground cinnamon
2 tablespoons chopped fresh parsley

Slice tops from tomatoes, scoop out seeds and discard seeds.

Heat oil in pan, add onion and garlic, cook, stirring until onion is soft, add mince, cook, stirring, 1 minute, add turmeric, garam masala, sugar, rind and juice, cook, stirring 2 minutes.

Combine mince mixture, nuts, rice, wild rice, apples, cinnamon and parsley in bowl. Spoon mixture into tomatoes.

Just before serving, place tomatoes on oven tray, bake, uncovered, in moderate oven 10 minutes.

Serves 6.

- Filling can be prepared a day ahead.
- Storage: Covered, in refrigerator.
- Freeze: Not suitable.
- Microwave: Suitable.

OLIVE AND HERB BREAD

7g sachet dry yeast
1 teaspoon castor sugar
½ cup warm water
3 cups plain flour
¾ cup warm water, approximately, extra
1 egg yolk
½ teaspoon fine sea salt
½ teaspoon dried oregano leaves
½ teaspoon dried basil leaves

FILLING
400g (2½ cups) black olives, chopped
4 cloves garlic, crushed
1 teaspoon dried oregano leaves
1 teaspoon dried basil leaves

Lightly grease a 20cm x 30cm lamington pan, line base with paper, grease paper. Combine yeast, sugar and water in small bowl. Cover, stand in warm place about 10 minutes or until mixture is frothy.

Sift flour into large bowl, stir in yeast mixture and enough extra water to form a soft dough. Turn dough onto floured surface, knead about 10 minutes or until dough is smooth and elastic.

Return dough to large greased bowl, cover, stand in warm place about 30 minutes or until dough is double in size.

Turn dough onto lightly floured surface, knead until smooth. Divide dough in half, roll halves to 20cm x 30cm rectangles. Place half into prepared pan. Spread filling over dough, place remaining half of dough over filling. Pierce dough at 3cm intervals with skewer, stand, uncovered, in warm place about 30 minutes or until dough is risen to top of pan. Brush dough evenly with egg yolk, sprinkle with combined salt and herbs. Bake in moderately hot oven 15 minutes, reduce to moderate, bake further 15 minutes or until well browned and bread sounds hollow when tapped. Turn onto wire rack, cool before cutting.

Filling: Combine all ingredients in bowl, mix well.

Serves 8.

- Bread can be made a day ahead.
- Storage: Airtight container.
- Freeze: Suitable.
- Microwave: Not suitable.

LEFT: Clockwise from front: Rice Mould with Spicy Mayonnaise, Cauliflower Salad with Parmesan Dressing and Tomatoes with Nutty Wild Rice Seasoning.
ABOVE: Olive and Herb Bread.

Left: Plates and tablecloth from Mosmania

SPICY POTATO BAKE

¼ cup olive oil
200g pepperoni, chopped
1kg potatoes, sliced
1 onion, chopped
¼ teaspoon cracked black pepper

Heat oil in baking dish, add pepperoni, potatoes, onion and pepper, stir over heat until coated with oil. Bake, uncovered, in moderately hot oven 30 minutes, stir mixture, bake further 30 minutes or until potatoes are well browned and crisp.

Serves 6.

■ Recipe best made close to serving.
■ Freeze: Not suitable.
■ Microwave: Not suitable.

COUNTRY SALAD WITH GARLIC CROUTONS

1 long thin green cucumber
3 large tomatoes
1 red Spanish onion, thinly sliced
½ cup (16) pimiento stuffed green olives, halved

GARLIC CROUTONS
3 thick slices bread
¼ cup olive oil
1 clove garlic, crushed

DRESSING
⅓ cup olive oil
2 tablespoons white vinegar
1 teaspoon dried mixed herbs
1 teaspoon honey

Run a fork lengthways down skin of cucumber, cut cucumber into thin slices. Cut tomatoes into wedges. Combine cucumber, tomatoes, onion, olives, garlic croutons and dressing in bowl; toss lightly to combine.

Garlic Croutons: Remove crusts from bread, brush bread with combined oil and garlic, cut bread into cubes. Spread cubes in single layer on oven tray, toast in moderately hot oven about 10 minutes or until lightly browned; cool.

Dressing: Combine all ingredients in jar; shake well.

Serves 6.

CHICK PEAS WITH PEPPERONI AND BACON

1½ cups (300g) chick peas
1¾ litres (7 cups) water
80g butter
1 large onion, sliced
4 bacon rashers, chopped
2 cloves garlic, crushed
250g pepperoni, sliced
2 tablespoons chopped fresh parsley
410g can tomatoes
1 tablespoon chopped fresh parsley, extra

Combine chickpeas with water in bowl, cover, stand overnight.

Transfer undrained chickpeas to pan, bring to boil, simmer, covered, about an hour or until tender; drain.

Heat butter in pan, add onion, bacon and garlic, cook, stirring, until onion is soft, add pepperoni, parsley and undrained crushed tomatoes, bring to boil, simmer, covered, 15 minutes. Serve sprinkled with extra parsley.

Serves 8.

- ■ Recipe can be made a day ahead.
- ■ Storage: Covered, in refrigerator.
- ■ Freeze: Not suitable.
- ■ Microwave: Not suitable.

- ■ Croutons can be made 2 days ahead. Assemble salad close to serving.
- ■ Storage: Croutons, in airtight container.
- ■ Freeze: Not suitable.
- ■ Microwave: Not suitable.

ABOVE: From left: Spicy Potato Bake, Country Salad with Garlic Croutons. RIGHT: Chickpeas with Pepperoni and Bacon.

Above: Glass and cloth from Mosmania; salad dish from Corso de Fiori. Right: Plate from Sandy de Beyer; tiles from Country Floors

GREEN VEGETABLES WITH PINE NUTS AND RAISINS

1/3 cup raisins, chopped
1/4 cup orange juice
1/4 cup olive oil
1 onion, chopped
2 cloves garlic, crushed
250g broccoli, chopped
100g snow peas
1 bunch (40 leaves) English spinach
1/2 cup pine nuts, toasted
2 teaspoons grated orange rind
1 teaspoon seasoned pepper
1/2 teaspoon celery salt

Combine raisins and juice in bowl, stand 30 minutes. Heat oil in large pan or wok, add onion and garlic, cook, stirring, until onion is soft. Add broccoli and snow peas, stir-fry, about 2 minutes or until just tender. Add raisin mixture and remaining ingredients to pan, stir-fry about 2 minutes or until heated through.

Serves 4.

■ Recipe best made close to serving.
■ Freeze: Not suitable.
■ Microwave: Suitable.

POTATO AND ORANGE SALAD

4 large (about 1¼kg) potatoes
200g green beans, chopped
1 red pepper
3 oranges, segmented
1 small red Spanish onion, thinly sliced
1/4 cup chopped fresh chives

DRESSING
2 tablespoons red wine vinegar
1/4 cup olive oil
1/4 teaspoon cracked black peppercorns

Boil, steam or microwave potatoes until just tender, drain, cool; cut into 2cm cubes. Boil, steam or microwave beans until just tender, drain; cool. Quarter pepper, remove seeds and membrane. Grill pepper, skin side up, until skin blisters. Peel skin, cut pepper into 1cm strips.

Combine potatoes, beans, pepper, oranges, onion, chives and dressing in bowl; cover, refrigerate several hours.
Dressing: Combine all ingredients in jar; shake well.

Serves 6.

■ Recipe can be made 3 hours ahead.
■ Storage: Covered, in refrigerator.
■ Freeze: Not suitable.
■ Microwave: Potatoes and beans suitable.

RICE AND ZUCCHINI GRATIN

1kg zucchini, sliced
50g butter
1 small onion, chopped
1 tablespoon chopped fresh parsley
1/2 cup rice
1 cup boiling water
1 egg white
2/3 cup sour cream
1 teaspoon seeded mustard
2 eggs, lightly beaten
2 tablespoons grated parmesan cheese

Grease a 15cm x 25cm loaf pan, line base with paper, grease paper.

Boil, steam or microwave zucchini until tender, drain. Heat butter in pan, add onion, cook, stirring until soft, add parsley, rice and water. Bring to boil, simmer, covered, about 15 minutes or until rice is tender and water is absorbed.

Remove pan from heat, stir in egg white. Press rice mixture into prepared pan, top with zucchini. Place sour cream in bowl, stir in mustard, eggs and cheese, stir until combined. Pour cream mixture over zucchini, bake uncovered in moderate oven about 45 minutes or until set and lightly browned.

Serves 4 to 6.

■ Recipe can be made a day ahead.
■ Storage: Covered, in refrigerator.
■ Freeze: Not suitable.
■ Microwave: Suitable.

CAPONATA

2 small (about 500g) eggplants
coarse cooking salt
½ cup olive oil
5 medium (600g) onions, chopped
2 cloves garlic, crushed
2 sticks celery, chopped
185g (1 cup) green olives, pitted, halved
2 x 410g cans tomatoes
1 teaspoon cracked black peppercorns
1 tablespoon sugar
½ cup red wine vinegar
2 tablespoons drained capers
1 tablespoon chopped fresh parsley
1 tablespoon chopped fresh basil

Chop eggplants into 2cm cubes, place in bowl sprinkle with salt; stand 1 hour.

Rinse eggplant cubes under cold water, pat dry with absorbent paper.

Heat oil in pan, add eggplant cubes, cook, stirring, until lightly browned; remove from pan. Add onions and garlic to pan, cook, covered, over low heat about 10 minutes or until onions are very soft. Stir in celery, olives, undrained crushed tomatoes and peppercorns. Bring to boil, simmer, uncovered, about 10 minutes or until celery is soft. Stir in sugar, vinegar and capers, simmer, uncovered, until almost all liquid has evaporated. Stir in eggplant cubes and herbs, cool; cover, refrigerate.

Serves 6.

■ Recipe can be made 2 days ahead.
■ Storage: Covered, in refrigerator.
■ Freeze: Not suitable.
■ Microwave: Not suitable.

LEFT: Clockwise from top left: Green Vegetables with Pine Nuts and Raisins, Potato and Orange Salad.
ABOVE: From left: Rice and Zucchini Gratin, Caponata.

Above: Dish and copperware from Corso De Fiori

93

RATATOUILLE

1 large (about 500g) eggplant
coarse cooking salt
6 small (about 350g) zucchini, sliced
1 red pepper, sliced
1 green pepper, sliced
1 yellow pepper, sliced
¼ cup olive oil
1 tablespoon olive oil, extra
2 onions, chopped
3 large tomatoes, peeled, seeded
2 cloves garlic, crushed
½ teaspoon sugar
1 tablespoon tomato paste
1 teaspoon chopped fresh parsley
1 teaspoon chopped fresh thyme
2 tablespoons shredded fresh
    basil leaves

Cut eggplant into 1½cm cubes. Place in bowl, sprinkle with salt, stand 30 minutes. Rinse eggplant under cold water, pat dry with absorbent paper. Fry eggplant, zucchini and peppers separately in the oil until lightly browned; drain on absorbent paper.

Heat extra oil in pan, add onions, cook, stirring until soft. Add chopped tomatoes, garlic, sugar, paste, parsley and thyme, bring to boil, simmer, uncovered, about 20 minutes or until thick. Stir eggplant, zucchini, peppers and basil into tomato mixture, reheat. Serve hot as an accompaniment or cold as a salad.

Serves 6.

- Recipe can be made 2 days ahead.
- Storage: Covered, in refrigerator.
- Freeze: Not suitable
- Microwave: Not suitable.

SALAD NICOISE

150g green beans
150g baby potatoes
56g can rolled fillets of anchovies,
    drained, rinsed
⅓ cup black olives, halved
12 cherry tomatoes, halved
6 lettuce leaves
425g can chunky tuna, drained

FRENCH DRESSING
¼ cup olive oil
1½ tablespoons lemon juice
1 teaspoon white vinegar
1 teaspoon seasoned pepper
1 teaspoon chopped fresh
    thyme leaves

Cut beans into 4cm lengths. Boil, steam or microwave beans and potatoes separately, until just tender; drain.

Slice potatoes, combine in bowl with beans, anchovies, olives, tomatoes, torn lettuce leaves and tuna.

Just before serving, toss lightly with dressing.

Dressing: Combine all ingredients in jar; shake well.

Serves 4.

- Recipe is best made close to serving.
- Freeze: Not suitable.
- Microwave: Vegetables suitable.

GARLIC AND HERB ARTICHOKES

4 fresh artichokes
½ cup pine nuts, chopped
⅓ cup chopped fresh parsley
⅓ cup chopped fresh mint
4 cloves garlic, crushed
⅓ cup olive oil

Trim artichoke stalks to 1cm, remove tough outer leaves, trim tops of leaves with scissors. Place artichokes in pan, cover with water, bring to boil, simmer, covered, about 30 minutes or until artichokes are tender; drain. Combine nuts, herbs, garlic and oil in bowl, spoon small amounts of mixture between leaves; wrap artichokes separately in foil.

Just before serving, place artichokes in ovenproof dish, bake, uncovered, in moderate oven about 20 minutes or until heated through.

Serves 4.

- Recipe can be prepared 6 hours ahead.
- Storage: Wrapped, in refrigerator.
- Freeze: Not suitable.
- Microwave: Artichokes suitable.

LEFT: From back: Salad Nicoise, Ratatouille.
ABOVE: Garlic and Herb Artichokes.

Left: Dishes and olive oil can from Accoutrement; cloth from Les Olivades

spinach, pimientos, nuts and pepper-corns, cook, stirring, until spinach is wilted. Serves 4.

- Recipe is best made close to serving.
- Freeze: Not suitable.
- Microwave: Not suitable.

POTATO, TUNA AND BEAN SALAD

10 (500g) baby new potatoes, quartered
425g can tuna, drained
310g can 4 bean mix, rinsed, drained

DRESSING
½ cup olive oil
50g can rolled fillets of anchovies
3 green shallots, chopped
1 tablespoon drained capers
1 tablespoon chopped fresh parsley
1½ tablespoons lemon juice

GOATS' CHEESE SALAD

6 bacon rashers, chopped
6 slices white bread
90g butter, melted
2 cloves garlic, crushed
lettuce

GOATS' CHEESE
250g goats' cheese
plain flour
2 eggs, lightly beaten
1 tablespoon milk
1 cup (70g) stale breadcrumbs
oil for deep-frying

VINAIGRETTE
⅓ cup olive oil
2 tablespoons white vinegar
½ teaspoon sugar
½ teaspoon seeded mustard
1 tablespoon chopped fresh chives

Add bacon to pan, cook, stirring, until bacon is crisp; drain on absorbent paper. Remove crusts from bread, brush bread with combined butter and garlic. Cut bread into 1cm cubes, spread in a single layer on oven tray, toast in moderate oven about 10 minutes.

Combine bacon, croutons, lettuce and cheese in bowl, sprinkle with vinaigrette.
Goats' Cheese: Cut cheese into wedges, toss in flour, then coat in combined egg

and milk, toss in breadcrumbs; cover, refrigerate 1 hour.
Just before serving, deep-fry wedges in hot oil until lightly browned; drain on absorbent paper.
Vinaigrette: Combine all ingredients in jar; shake well.

Serves 4.

- Recipe can be prepared a day ahead.
- Storage: Cheese, covered, in refrigerator; croutons, in airtight container; bacon, covered, in refrigerator; vinaigrette, in screw-top jar.
- Freeze: Not suitable.
- Microwave: Not suitable.

SPINACH WITH ONIONS AND PIMIENTO

2 tablespoons olive oil
2 red Spanish onions, sliced
2 cloves garlic, crushed
1 bunch (40 leaves) English spinach, shredded
½ cup canned pimientos, drained, sliced
½ cup pine nuts, toasted
½ teaspoon cracked black peppercorns

Heat oil in pan, add onions and garlic, cook, stirring, over low heat about 10 minutes or until onions are very soft. Stir in

Boil, steam or microwave potatoes until tender. Combine potatoes, tuna, beans and hot dressing in large bowl; mix well.
Dressing: Heat oil in pan, add undrained anchovies and shallots, cook, stirring, about 1 minute or until shallots are soft. Add remaining ingredients, cook, stirring, 3 minutes.
Serves 6.

- Recipe can be prepared 4 hours ahead
- Freeze: Not suitable.
- Microwave: Potatoes suitable.

SAUTEED PEPPER AND SALAMI SALAD

1 large red pepper
1 large green pepper
1 large yellow pepper
¼ cup olive oil
2 cloves garlic, crushed
½ teaspoon chopped fresh thyme
100g sliced salami
1 mignonette lettuce
½ bunch curly endive
½ cup shredded fresh basil leaves

DRESSING
2 tablespoons olive oil
1 tablespoon lemon juice
¼ teaspoon ground black pepper
2 cloves garlic, crushed

Cut peppers into diamond shapes. Heat oil in pan, add peppers, garlic and thyme, cook, stirring, 2 minutes. Cover, cook over low heat about 5 minutes or until peppers are just tender; cool.

Cut salami into 5mm strips. Combine salami, pepper mixture, lettuce, endive and basil in bowl.
Just before serving, pour over dressing.
Dressing: Combine all ingredients in jar; shake well.
Serves 6.

- Recipe can be prepared 4 hours ahead.
- Storage: Covered, in refrigerator.
- Freeze: Not suitable.
- Microwave: Not suitable.

LEFT: Goats' Cheese Salad.
BELOW: Clockwise from left: Spinach with Onions and Pimiento, Potato, Tuna and Bean Salad, Sauteed Pepper and Salami Salad.

Below: Plates from Lifestyle Imports; wok from Corso de Fiori

CAKES & DESSERTS

Sweet treats which we have chosen from the Mediterranean region will both delight and tempt you. You'll love the varied selection to serve after dinner or with coffee, such as sesame seed balls, baklava, almond nougat, toffee almonds and fried pastries with currants. There are cakes and pastries galore, as well as slices, cheesecakes, biscuits, ice-creams, shortbread, meringues, and mousses. Most can be prepared ahead and suit any season, from the rich sweet zabaglione to the light summery citrus-flavoured mint sorbet.

CHESTNUT WHISKY CHARLOTTE

250g packet sponge finger biscuits

WHISKY SYRUP
½ cup castor sugar
¼ cup water
¼ cup whisky

CHESTNUT CREAM FILLING
3 egg yolks
½ cup castor sugar
¾ cup milk
3cm piece vanilla bean, split
227g can sweetened chestnut puree
1 tablespoon gelatine
2 tablespoons water
300ml carton thickened cream

Line base of a charlotte or straight-sided mould (6 cup capacity) with greaseproof paper. Dip sponge fingers quickly into whisky syrup, line side of mould with sponge fingers, trim to fit together. Dip remaining sponge fingers in syrup, trim to cover base of mould.

Pour filling into prepared mould, cover, refrigerate until firm. Serve decorated with extra whipped cream, cherries and chocolate shavings if desired.

Syrup: Combine sugar and water in pan, stir over heat until sugar is dissolved, bring to boil, simmer without stirring, 1 minute, stir in whisky; cool.

Chestnut Cream Filling: Combine egg yolks and sugar in small heatproof bowl, beat with electric mixer until thick and creamy. Heat milk and vanilla bean in pan, bring to boil, remove from heat; discard vanilla bean. Gradually beat hot milk into egg mixture while motor is operating.

Place bowl over pan of simmering water, stir custard mixture over water about 10 minutes or until mixture has thickened slightly.

Remove from heat, stir in chestnut puree, stir until smooth.

Sprinkle gelatine over water in cup, stand in pan of simmering water, stir until dissolved. Stir gelatine mixture into chestnut mixture. Beat cream in small bowl until firm peaks form, fold into chestnut mixture.

Serves 8.

- Charlotte can be made 3 days ahead.
- Storage: Covered, in refrigerator.
- Freeze: Not suitable.
- Microwave: Gelatine suitable.

SOFT RASPBERRY MERINGUES WITH TWO SAUCES

125g frozen raspberries, thawed
1 cup castor sugar
½ cup water
4 egg whites
2 tablespoons castor sugar, extra

RASPBERRY SAUCE
200g frozen raspberries, thawed
½ teaspoon cornflour
½ teaspoon water

WHITE CHOCOLATE SAUCE
100g white chocolate, melted
1 cup thickened cream

Blend or process raspberries until smooth, strain. Combine sugar and water in pan, stir over heat, without boiling, until sugar is dissolved. Add raspberry puree to pan, bring to boil, boil, uncovered, without stirring, about 10 minutes or until a drop of syrup forms a hard ball when dropped into a glass of cold water (122° C using candy thermometer).

Beat egg whites in small bowl until soft peaks form, gradually beat in extra sugar, beat until dissolved. Gradually beat in hot syrup in a thin stream while motor is operating, beat until mixture is cool.

Spoon mixture into piping bag fitted with star tube, pipe 5cm rosettes on oven tray covered with baking paper. Bake in slow oven 35 minutes. Stand 3 minutes before peeling paper away. Serve immediately with both sauces.

Raspberry Sauce: Blend or process raspberries until smooth, strain. Combine raspberry puree with blended cornflour and water in pan, stir over heat until sauce boils and thickens.

White Chocolate Sauce: Combine chocolate and cream in bowl, beat with wooden spoon until smooth.

Serves 8.

- Sauces can be made a day ahead.
- Storage: Covered, in refrigerator.
- Freeze: Not suitable.
- Microwave: Sauces suitable.

LEFT: From left: Chestnut Whisky Charlotte, Soft Raspberry Meringues with Two Sauces.

CHOCOLATE APRICOT TRIFLE CAKE

250g packet sponge finger biscuits
1 cup castor sugar
½ cup water
3½ cups (700g) ricotta cheese
¼ cup chopped pistachios
200g dark chocolate, finely chopped
¾ cup chopped glace apricots
½ teaspoon vanilla essence
¼ teaspoon ground cinnamon

GLAZE
¼ cup apricot jam, warmed
1½ tablespoons icing sugar

Grease a 25cm springform tin, line base with paper, grease paper. Trim biscuits level with top of tin; line side of tin with biscuits. Crush remaining biscuits, spread over base of tin.

Combine sugar and water in pan, stir over heat, without boiling, until sugar is dissolved. Bring to boil, boil, uncovered, 2 minutes; cool.

Press cheese through sieve into large bowl, add sugar syrup, nuts, chocolate, apricots, essence and cinnamon; mix well. Pour into prepared pan, cover, refrigerate until set.

Brush glaze over cake, refrigerate until set. Decorate cake with whipped cream, extra chopped glace apricots and chopped pistachios if desired.

Glaze: Strain jam into pan, stir in sifted icing sugar, stir over heat until combined.

Serves 6 to 8.

- Recipe can be made a day ahead.
- Storage: Covered, in refrigerator.
- Freeze: Not suitable.
- Microwave: Glaze suitable.

SESAME HONEY PUFFS

1 teaspoon dry yeast
½ teaspoon castor sugar
1½ cups plain flour
1 cup warm water
oil for deep-frying
2 cups honey
2 tablespoons sesame seeds, toasted
2 teaspoons ground cinnamon

Combine yeast and sugar in small bowl with 2 tablespoons of the flour; stir in water, cover, stand in warm place about 15 minutes or until mixture is frothy.

Sift remaining flour into large bowl, stir in yeast mixture, mix to a smooth batter. Cover bowl, stand in warm place about 1 hour or until batter is doubled in size and bubbles appear on surface.

Deep-fry dessertspoons of mixture in hot oil until puffs are light brown; drain on wire rack, transfer to bowl.

Heat honey in pan until runny, pour over puffs in bowl, sprinkle with combined seeds and cinnamon.

Serves 6 to 8.

- Recipe best made close to serving.
- Freeze: Not suitable.
- Microwave: Honey suitable.

COCONUT PISTACHIO ICE-CREAM

½ cup castor sugar
1 tablespoon cornflour
2 x 150g cans coconut milk
4 eggs, lightly beaten
300ml carton thickened cream
½ cup chopped pistachios

Combine sugar with blended cornflour and coconut milk in pan, stir over heat until mixture boils and thickens; cool slightly. Stir in combined eggs and cream, stir over heat without boiling until mixture thickens slightly; cool. Pour cream mixture into loaf pan, cover, freeze until firm.

Remove ice-cream from pan, beat in large bowl with electric mixer until smooth; fold in nuts. Return mixture to pan, cover, freeze until firm. Stand at room temperature 20 minutes before serving.

Serves 4.

- Recipe can be made 3 days ahead.
- Storage: Covered, in freezer.
- Microwave: Not suitable.

LEFT: Clockwise from top: Chocolate Apricot Trifle Cake, Coconut Pistachio Ice-cream, Sesame Honey Puffs.

Plates from Lifestyle Imports; fabric from Redelman Fabrics; ornaments from The Parterre Garden

FROZEN FRUITY CASSATA CAKE

1 cup (200g) ricotta cheese
½ cup castor sugar
1½ tablespoons thickened cream
50g dark chocolate, finely chopped
1 tablespoon finely chopped
    pistachios
¼ cup finely chopped glace apricots
¼ cup finely chopped glace pineapple
2 tablespoons finely chopped
    glace cherries
¼ teaspoon ground cinnamon
3 teaspoons Maraschino
17cm round sponge cake
2 tablespoons Maraschino, extra

Press cheese through sieve into large bowl, stir in sugar, cream, chocolate, nuts, fruit, cinnamon and liqueur; mix well.

Line a 8cm x 26cm bar pan with foil, brush with some of the extra liqueur.

Slice sponge into 1cm thick slices. Trim slices to line base and sides of prepared pan, brush with a little more extra liqueur. Spoon cheese mixture into pan, top with cake, brush with remaining extra liqueur. Cover with foil, freeze until firm.

Stand cake 10 minutes at room temperature before slicing.

Serves 6.

■ Recipe can be made 3 days ahead.
■ Storage: Covered, in freezer.
■ Microwave: Not suitable

CREAMY DOUBLE CHOCOLATE BAVAROIS

2 cups milk
4 egg yolks
½ cup castor sugar
1 tablespoon gelatine
¼ cup water
150g white chocolate, melted
150g milk chocolate, melted
3 teaspoons dark rum
300ml carton thickened cream

Lightly oil 6 moulds (1 cup capacity). Heat milk in pan, bring to boil, remove from heat. Beat egg yolks and sugar until light and fluffy. Gradually beat hot milk into egg mixture. Sprinkle gelatine over water in cup, stand in small pan of simmering water, stir until dissolved; cool slightly.

Stir gelatine mixture into custard. Divide mixture into 2 portions, stir white chocolate into 1 portion and milk chocolate and rum into remaining portion, cool to room temperature.

Beat cream in small bowl until soft peaks form. Fold half the cream into each chocolate mixture. Drop spoonfuls of each chocolate mixture alternately into the prepared moulds, swirl lightly with a knife; cover, refrigerate until firm.

Serves 6.

■ Moulds can be made 3 days ahead.
■ Storage: Covered, in refrigerator.
■ Freeze: Not suitable.
■ Microwave: Gelatine suitable.

ALMOND APRICOT FLAN

1¾ cups plain flour
½ cup castor sugar
125g butter, chopped
1 egg, lightly beaten
icing sugar

APRICOT FILLING
¾ cup chopped dried apricots
1 cup hot water
¼ cup plain flour
¼ cup self-raising flour
½ cup packaged ground almonds
⅓ cup castor sugar
3 eggs, lightly beaten
¼ cup milk
2 teaspoons almond essence

Lightly grease a 24cm flan tin. Sift flour and sugar into bowl, rub in butter, add egg, mix to a firm dough. Press dough into ball, knead gently on floured surface until smooth, cover, refrigerate 30 minutes.

Roll dough on lightly floured surface large enough to line prepared tin, trim edges. Place tin on oven tray, line pastry with paper, fill with dried beans or rice. Bake in moderately hot oven 10 minutes, remove paper and beans, bake further 10 minutes or until lightly browned; cool.

Pour filling into pastry case, bake in moderate oven about 25 minutes or until firm. Sprinkle lightly with sifted icing sugar.

Apricot Filling: Combine apricots with hot water in bowl; stand 30 minutes, drain. Combine sifted flours, almonds and sugar in bowl. Stir in combined eggs, milk and essence; mix well, stir in apricots.

Serves 6 to 8.

■ Recipe can be made a day ahead.
■ Storage: Covered, in refrigerator.
■ Freeze: Not suitable.

RIGHT: Clockwise from top: Almond Apricot Flan, Creamy Double Chocolate Bavarois, Frozen Fruity Cassata Cake.

Fabric from Redelman Fabrics

APPLE AND ORANGE TART WITH SPICED CREAM

2 cups plain flour
¼ teaspoon ground cinnamon
125g butter, chopped
1 tablespoon castor sugar
1 egg, separated
¼ cup water, approximately
icing sugar

FILLING
60g butter
4 large (about 1kg) apples,
  peeled, grated
3 teaspoons grated orange rind
¼ cup orange juice
¼ cup castor sugar
2 tablespoons honey

SPICED CREAM
300ml carton thickened cream
½ teaspoon ground cinnamon
¼ teaspoon ground nutmeg

Sift flour and cinnamon into bowl, rub in butter, stir in sugar. Add egg yolk and enough water to form a firm dough. Press dough into ball, knead gently on lightly floured surface until smooth, cover, refrigerate 30 minutes.

Roll two-thirds of dough between sheets of greaseproof paper large enough to line deep 24cm flan tin. Lift pastry into tin gently, ease into side, trim edge. Place tin on oven tray, line pastry with paper, fill with dried beans or rice. Bake in moderately hot oven 10 minutes, remove paper and beans, bake further 10 minutes or until lightly browned; cool.

Spoon filling into pastry case. Roll remaining dough to 2mm thick, cut into 1cm strips. Lay pastry strips over filling to form lattice, trim edges. Brush pastry with lightly beaten egg white, bake in moderately hot oven about 30 minutes or until lightly browned. Serve with spiced cream; dust with sifted icing sugar.

Filling: Heat butter in pan, add apples, rind, juice and sugar. Cook, stirring, about 5 minutes or until apples begin to brown and liquid is evaporated. Remove from heat, cool. Drain apples well; stir in honey.

Spiced Cream: Beat all ingredients in small bowl until soft peaks form.

Serves 6 to 8.

■ Recipe can be made a day ahead.
■ Storage: Covered, in refrigerator.
■ Freeze: Not suitable.
■ Microwave: Not suitable.

CHOCOLATE CHIFFON TERRINE

3 teaspoons gelatine
1½ tablespoons water
200g milk chocolate, melted
2 eggs, separated
2 tablespoons sweet sherry
300ml carton thickened cream
250g packet sponge finger biscuits
¾ cup milk

Line a 14cm x 21cm loaf pan with foil. Sprinkle gelatine over water in cup, stand in small pan of simmering water, stir until dissolved; cool slightly.

Combine gelatine mixture, chocolate, egg yolks and sherry in bowl; stir in cream, refrigerate until just beginning to set. Beat egg whites in small bowl until soft peaks form, fold gently into chocolate mixture in 2 batches.

Trim about 5 biscuits to fit base of prepared pan, dip biscuits into milk, place in pan. Spoon over one-third of the chocolate mixture. Repeat layers, trimming biscuits when necessary, finishing with chocolate layer. Cover pan, refrigerate until set.

Serves 8.

■ Recipe can be made a day ahead.
■ Storage: Covered, in refrigerator.
■ Freeze: Not suitable.
■ Microwave: Gelatine and chocolate suitable.

LEMON AND MINT SORBET

3 cups water
1 cup castor sugar
2 cups lemon juice
½ cup cream
2 tablespoons chopped fresh mint

Combine water and sugar in pan, stir over heat, without boiling, until sugar is dissolved. Bring to boil, simmer, uncovered, 10 minutes, without stirring; cool.

Stir juice and cream into sugar syrup, pour into lamington pan; cover, freeze several hours or until firm.

Remove mixture from pan, beat with electric mixer in bowl until smooth, stir in mint. Return mixture to pan; cover, freeze until firm.

Serves 6.

■ Recipe can be made 3 days ahead.
■ Storage: Covered, in freezer.
■ Microwave: Not suitable.

ABOVE: Chocolate Chiffon Terrine.
RIGHT: From top: Lemon and Mint Sorbet, Apple and Orange Tart with Spiced Cream.

China from Butler & Co/Zuhause

PECAN CREPE STACK

½ cup plain flour
2 eggs, lightly beaten
1 cup milk
2 teaspoons oil

CARAMEL PECAN FILLING
2 cups brown sugar, firmly packed
300ml carton thickened cream
1½ cups (190g) chopped pecan nuts
⅔ cup chopped dates
2 tablespoons Grand Marnier

Sift flour into bowl, gradually stir in combined eggs, milk and oil, beat until smooth, cover, stand 30 minutes.

Pour 2 to 3 tablespoons of batter into heated greased heavy-based crepe pan, cook until lightly browned underneath. Turn crepe, brown other side. Repeat with remaining batter. You will need 9 crepes for this recipe.

Just before serving, lightly grease a 20cm springform tin. Place a crepe in tin, top with a layer of filling, continue layering with remaining crepes and filling, finishing with a layer of filling. Cover tin with foil, place on oven tray, bake in moderate oven about 20 minutes or until heated through.

Caramel Pecan Filling: Combine sugar and cream in pan, stir over heat, without boiling, until sugar is dissolved. Bring to boil, boil, uncovered, 2 minutes, remove from heat; stir in nuts, dates and liqueur.

Serves 6.

- Recipe can be prepared a day ahead.
- Storage: Crepes, layered with paper, covered, in refrigerator. Caramel pecan filling, covered in refrigerator.
- Freeze: Cooked crepes suitable.
- Microwave: Suitable.

PEACH AND RICOTTA ICE-CREAM

250g dried peaches
1 cup boiling water
825g can peaches in syrup
1¼ cups (250g) ricotta cheese
¼ cup castor sugar
2 teaspoons gelatine
1 tablespoon water
apricot food colouring
300ml carton thickened cream

Combine dried peaches with boiling water in bowl; cover, stand 1 hour.

Drain dried peaches. Blend or process undrained canned peaches, cheese and sugar until smooth. Sprinkle gelatine over water in cup; stand in small pan of simmering water, stir until dissolved. Stir gelatine mixture into peach mixture, tint with a little food colouring if desired; mix

ZABAGLIONE

8 egg yolks
¾ cup castor sugar
1 cup marsala
250g punnet strawberries, sliced

Beat egg yolks and sugar in top half of double saucepan or heatproof bowl with electric mixer until pale and creamy, gradually beat in marsala.

Place mixture over pan of simmering water, continue to beat with electric mixer for about 10 minutes or until mixture is thick and creamy. Fold in strawberries, pour into glasses.

Serves 6.

■ Recipe best made just before serving.
■ Freeze: Not suitable.
■ Microwave: Not suitable.

well. Pour mixture into lamington pan, cover, freeze about 2 hours or until mixture is just firm.

Remove ice-cream from pan, blend or process until thick and creamy. Beat cream in small bowl until soft peaks form, fold cream into peach mixture. Return mixture to pan, cover, freeze until firm.

Serves 6 to 8.

■ Recipe can be made 3 days ahead.
■ Storage: Covered, in freezer.
■ Microwave: Gelatine suitable.

ABOVE: From left: Pecan Crepe Stack, Peach and Ricotta Ice-cream
RIGHT: Zabaglione

Right: Glasses from Corso de Fiori; fabric from Redelman Fabrics

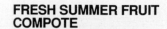

APRICOT GLAZED GRAPE TART

1 cup plain flour
¼ cup castor sugar
90g butter
1 egg yolk
2 teaspoons milk, approximately
500g white seedless grapes

FILLING
250g packet cream cheese
2 tablespoons Grand Marnier
¼ cup orange juice
¾ cup icing sugar
½ cup thickened cream

GLAZE
¼ cup apricot jam
1 teaspoon cornflour
2 tablespoons water

Lightly grease a deep 22cm flan tin. Sift flour and sugar into bowl, rub in butter. Add egg yolk and enough milk to form a firm dough. Press dough into ball, knead gently on lightly floured surface until smooth, cover, refrigerate 30 minutes.

Roll dough between sheets of greaseproof paper large enough to line prepared tin; trim edges. Line pastry with paper, fill with dried beans or rice. Bake in moderate oven 10 minutes, remove paper and beans, bake further 10 minutes or until light brown; cool.

Spoon filling into pastry case, refrigerate 30 minutes. Place grapes over filling, brush with glaze, refrigerate.

Filling: Beat cheese in small bowl until smooth, gradually add liqueur, juice and sifted icing sugar, beat until smooth. Beat cream in small bowl until soft peaks form, fold into cheese mixture.

Glaze: Sieve jam into pan, stir in blended cornflour and water, stir over heat until mixture boils and thickens slightly. Cool 10 minutes before using.

Serves 6 to 8.

■ Recipe can be made a day ahead.
■ Storage: Covered, in refrigerator.
■ Freeze: Not suitable.
■ Microwave: Glaze suitable.

FRESH SUMMER FRUIT COMPOTE

2 large firm peaches
4 firm apricots
4 firm plums
1 cup castor sugar
1 teaspoon grated lemon rind
2 tablespoons lemon juice
1 cup orange juice

Peel and stone fruit. Cut peaches into quarters, halve apricots and plums. Place fruit into shallow dish.

Combine sugar, rind and juices in pan, stir over heat without boiling, until sugar is dissolved; bring to boil. Pour syrup over fruit; cover, cool.

Drain syrup mixture from fruit, reserve fruit. Bring syrup to boil in pan, simmer, uncovered, about 10 minutes or until reduced by half. Pour hot syrup over reserved fruit; cool. Refrigerate fruit before serving.

Serves 4.

■ Recipe can be made a week ahead.
■ Storage: Covered, in refrigerator.
■ Freeze: Not suitable.
■ Microwave: Syrup suitable.

CARAMEL CHEESECAKE

⅓ cup castor sugar
⅓ cup water
⅓ cup milk
½ cup castor sugar, extra
2 cups (400g) ricotta cheese
1 teaspoon grated lemon rind
4 eggs

Combine sugar and water in pan, stir over heat, without boiling, until sugar is dissolved. Bring to boil, boil, uncovered, without stirring, until sugar syrup is golden brown. Pour caramel into 20cm round cake pan, swirl to coat base evenly.

Combine milk and extra sugar in pan, stir over heat, without boiling, until sugar is dissolved; cool.

Press cheese through sieve into large bowl. Beat cheese with electric mixer until smooth, gradually beat in milk mixture and rind, beat until combined. Gradually add eggs, 1 at a time, beat well between additions. Pour mixture into prepared pan, place pan in baking dish with enough boiling water to come halfway up side of pan. Bake, uncovered, in moderate oven about 1 hour or until set. Cool in pan, cover, refrigerate several hours or overnight before turning out.

Serves 6 to 8.

■ Recipe best made a day ahead.
■ Storage: Covered, in refrigerator.
■ Freeze: Not suitable.
■ Microwave: Not suitable.

LEFT: From top: Apricot Glazed Grape Tart, Fresh Summer Fruit Compote.
ABOVE RIGHT: Clockwise from top: Chocolate Orange Mousse, Layered Fruit Pudding, Caramel Cheesecake.

Above right: China from Butler & Co/Zuhause

LAYERED FRUIT PUDDING

½ cup chopped dried apricots
½ cup chopped raisins
¼ cup chopped dried apple
¼ cup chopped dried dates
¼ cup chopped dried mango
¼ cup chopped dried paw paw
½ cup rum
17cm stale round sponge cake
4 eggs, lightly beaten
2 cups milk
¾ cup castor sugar

Combine fruit and rum in bowl; mix well, stand 2 hours.

Cut cake into 2cm cubes. Place half the cake cubes in single layer into greased shallow ovenproof dish (8 cup capacity), sprinkle with half the fruit. Repeat layering, ending with fruit. Pour over combined eggs, milk and sugar. Place dish in baking dish with enough boiling water to come halfway up side of ovenproof dish. Bake uncovered in moderate oven about 45 minutes or until firm.

Serves 6.

- ■ Recipe best made just before serving.
- ■ Freeze: Not suitable.
- ■ Microwave: Not suitable.

CHOCOLATE ORANGE MOUSSE

200g dark chocolate, melted
6 eggs, separated
½ cup sour cream
2 tablespoons Tia Maria or Kahlua
1 teaspoon grated orange rind
3 teaspoons gelatine
2 tablespoons water
300ml carton thickened cream

Combine chocolate, egg yolks, sour cream, liqueur and rind in bowl. Sprinkle gelatine over water in cup, stand in small pan of simmering water, stir until dissolved; stir into chocolate mixture.

Beat thickened cream in small bowl until soft peaks form. Fold cream into chocolate mixture. Beat egg whites in medium bowl until soft peaks form. Fold egg whites into chocolate mixture in 2 batches. Spoon mousse into 6 dishes (1 cup capacity); refrigerate until set. Top with blueberries dusted with icing sugar, if desired.

Serves 6.

- ■ Mousse can be made a day ahead.
- ■ Storage: Covered, in refrigerator.
- ■ Freeze: Not suitable.
- ■ Microwave: Chocolate and gelatine suitable.

EASY DRIED FRUIT SALAD

¾ cup sultanas
¾ cup prunes, halved
2 cups (300g) dried apricots, halved
**2½ cups (250g) coarsely chopped
    dried pears**
⅔ cup slivered almonds
1 teaspoon grated orange rind
¼ cup orange juice
1 teaspoon mixed spice
1 tablespoon sweet sherry
3½ cups water
⅓ cup castor sugar

Combine all ingredients in bowl; mix well. Cover, refrigerate 48 hours.

Serves 6 to 8.

■ Recipe can be made 4 days ahead.
■ Storage: Covered, in refrigerator.
■ Freeze: Not suitable.

CHESTNUT CREME CARAMEL

½ cup castor sugar
¼ cup water
5 eggs
2 tablespoons castor sugar, extra
¾ cup milk
¾ cup thickened cream
2 teaspoons rum
250g can sweetened chestnut puree

Combine sugar and water in pan, stir over heat, without boiling, until sugar is dissolved. Bring to boil, boil, uncovered, without stirring, about 5 minutes or until mixture is golden brown. Pour caramel evenly over base of deep 23cm round cake pan; cool.

Whisk eggs with extra sugar in bowl, whisk in milk, cream and rum, then chestnut puree. Pour custard into prepared pan, place pan in baking dish, pour in enough boiling water to come halfway up side of pan. Bake, uncovered in moderate oven about 50 minutes or until custard is set; cool. Refrigerate several hours or overnight before turning out; serve with whipped cream if desired.

Serves 6 to 8.

■ Recipe is best made a day ahead.
■ Storage: Covered, in refrigerator.
■ Freeze: Not suitable.
■ Microwave: Not suitable.

FRUITY CHEESECAKE

12 sheets fillo pastry
125g butter, melted
½ cup plain flour
¼ cup packaged ground almonds
¾ cup castor sugar
2 cups milk
6 eggs, lightly beaten
2½ cups (500g) ricotta cheese
½ cup sultanas
½ cup chopped dates
¼ cup Amaretto
2 teaspoons grated orange rind

Grease 20cm x 30cm lamington pan. Layer 6 of the pastry sheets together, brushing each with some melted butter,

place into prepared pan, leaving 2cm of pastry overhanging.

Blend flour, almonds and sugar with milk in pan, stir over heat until mixture boils and thickens; cool.

Transfer flour mixture to large bowl, beat in eggs and cheese with electric mixer. Stir in sultanas, dates, liqueur and rind. Pour mixture into prepared pan.

Layer remaining pastry sheets together, brushing each with more butter. Cut pastry to fit top of pan, place over cheese mixture, fold overhanging edges inwards; brush with remaining butter. Bake in moderate oven about 45 minutes or until light brown; cool before cutting.

Serves 6 to 8.

■ Recipe can be made 3 hours ahead.
■ Storage: Room temperature.
■ Freeze: Not suitable.
■ Microwave: Not suitable.

ABOVE: Fruity Cheesecake.
LEFT: From left: Chestnut Creme Caramel, Easy Dried Fruit Salad.

Above: Terracotta ornament from The Parterre Garden. Left: Plates from Lifestyle Imports; fabric from Redelman Fabrics.

CHOCOLATE ALMOND TART

1⅔ cups plain flour
2 tablespoons castor sugar
¼ cup packaged ground almonds
100g butter, chopped
1 egg yolk
½ teaspoon almond essence
2 tablespoons water, approximately

FILLING
1½ cups (220g) blanched almonds
150g dark chocolate, chopped
⅔ cup mixed peel, finely chopped
2 tablespoons rum
⅔ cup castor sugar
2 tablespoons thickened cream
3 eggs, lightly beaten
1 teaspoon almond essence

Lightly grease shallow 25cm flan tin. Sift flour into bowl, stir in sugar and almonds, rub in butter. Add egg yolk, essence and enough water to form a firm dough. Press dough into ball, knead gently on lightly floured surface until smooth, cover, refrigerate 30 minutes.

Roll dough on floured surface large enough to line prepared tin; trim edges. Line tin with paper, fill with dried beans or rice, bake in moderately hot oven 10 minutes, remove paper and beans, bake further 10 minutes or until lightly browned.

Spoon filling into pastry case. Bake in moderate oven about 30 minutes or until filling is set and lightly browned.

Filling: Blend or process almonds until finely chopped. Combine remaining ingredients in bowl, add almonds; mix well.

Serves 6 to 8.

- Recipe can be made a day ahead.
- Storage: Covered, in refrigerator.
- Freeze: Not suitable.
- Microwave: Not suitable.

CREAMY CHOCOLATE PRALINE

250g dark chocolate, melted
250g mascarpone cheese
300ml carton thickened cream

PRALINE
⅔ cup chopped roasted hazelnuts
1 cup castor sugar
1 cup water

CUSTARD CREAM
300ml carton thickened cream
1 teaspoon Creme de Cacao
4 egg yolks
¼ cup castor sugar
2 teaspoons cornflour
2 teaspoons water

Combine cooled chocolate with cheese in bowl; mix well. Beat cream in small bowl until soft peaks form; fold cream into chocolate mixture.

Divide chocolate mixture between 8 serving dishes (¾ cup capacity). Sprinkle each dish with 2 tablespoons of the crushed praline, top with custard cream, cover; refrigerate until firm. Serve topped with reserved praline.

Praline: Spread nuts evenly onto greased oven tray. Combine sugar and water in pan, stir over heat, without boiling, until sugar is dissolved. Bring to boil, boil, uncovered, without stirring, about 7 minutes or until sugar syrup is golden brown. Allow bubbles to subside, pour evenly over nuts. When toffee is set, break into pieces, reserve 8 pieces for decorating. Blend or process remaining toffee pieces until finely crushed.

Custard Cream: Heat cream and liqueur in pan until almost boiling. Beat yolks and sugar in small bowl with electric mixer until pale, gradually beat in hot cream mixture and blended cornflour and water. Return mixture to pan, stir over heat until mixture boils and thickens slightly; cover, cool; refrigerate before using.

Serves 8.

- Praline can be made 2 weeks ahead. Recipe can be made a day ahead.
- Storage: Praline, covered, at room temperature. Desserts, covered, in refrigerator.
- Freeze: Not suitable.
- Microwave: Not suitable.

LEFT: Chocolate Almond Tart.
BELOW: Creamy Chocolate Praline.

Left: Fabric from Redelman Fabrics

BAKLAVA

18 sheets fillo pastry
125g butter, melted
125g ghee, melted
1 tablespoon water

NUT MIXTURE
1½ cups (240g) blanched almonds,
    toasted, ground
1½ cups (150g) walnuts, ground
1 tablespoon castor sugar
½ teaspoon ground cinnamon
½ teaspoon mixed spice

SYRUP
2 cups castor sugar
1 cup water
1 cinnamon stick
1 tablespoon honey
2 cloves
½ teaspoon grated lemon rind

Grease a deep 19cm square cake pan.

Cut pastry roughly to size of pan. Layer 3 pastry sheets together with combined butter and ghee brushed on each layer; trim to fit into prepared pan. Sprinkle with one-fifth of the nut mixture. Continue layering with remaining buttered pastry and nut mixture, ending with buttered pastry. Use a sharp knife to cut part of the way through the layered pastry. Sprinkle baklava with water. Bake in moderate oven 30 minutes, reduce heat to slow, bake a further 10 minutes or until well browned. Pour hot syrup over hot baklava; cool in pan.

Nut Mixture: Combine all ingredients in bowl; mix well.

Syrup: Combine all ingredients in pan, stir over heat, without boiling, until sugar is dissolved. Bring to boil; boil, uncovered, without stirring, about 4 minutes or until slightly thickened. Discard spices.

■ Baklava can be made a week ahead.
■ Storage: Airtight container.
■ Freeze: Not suitable.
■ Microwave: Not suitable.

ALMOND NOUGAT

For best results, use a candy thermometer. The cooking times mentioned should be used only as a guide. Watch the syrup all the time during cooking as temperatures are critical.

4 sheets edible rice paper
1 cup castor sugar
¾ cup honey
1 tablespoon rose water
1 egg white
1 cup (160g) blanched almonds,
    toasted

Line a 23cm square slab pan with 2 sheets of rice paper.

Combine sugar, honey and rose water in pan. Stir over heat, without boiling, until sugar is dissolved. Bring to boil, simmer for about 4 minutes or until a teaspoon of sugar syrup dropped into a cup of cold water forms a soft ball and will just crack when broken with fingers (140°C on a candy thermometer or "small crack".)

Beat egg white in small bowl with electric mixer until firm peaks form, slowly pour in hot syrup, while motor is operating. Continue beating about 1 minute or until mixture is thick. Fold in almonds, spread into prepared pan, cover with remaining rice paper, cool in pan.

■ Recipe can be made 2 days ahead.
■ Storage: Airtight container.
■ Freeze: Not suitable.
■ Microwave: Not suitable.

RIGHT: From top: Almond Nougat, Baklava.

Fabric from Redelman Fabrics

SERPENT CAKE

**2½ cups (310g) packaged
  ground almonds**
1½ cups icing sugar
½ teaspoon grated lemon rind
2 tablespoons lemon juice
2 tablespoons orange juice
½ teaspoon almond essence
½ teaspoon vanilla essence
50g butter, melted
375g packet fillo pastry
125g butter, melted, extra
1 egg, lightly beaten
2 tablespoons water
icing sugar

Combine almonds, sifted icing sugar, rind, juices and essences in bowl, stir in butter. Refrigerate about 1 hour or until firm.

Roll mixture about 1cm thick and 5cm long. Layer 2 sheets of pastry with extra butter. Place almond mixture at 1cm intervals down long edge of pastry. Roll pastry tightly around mixture, tucking in ends while rolling. Repeat with remaining pastry, extra butter and almond mixture.

Cover oven tray with foil, grease well. Coil pastry mixture, starting from the centre and working out to edge of tray to form a spiral, brushing sides of mixture with combined egg and water as you work. Bake in moderate oven about 20 minutes or until lightly browned. Transfer cake to wire rack, return to moderate oven, bake further 10 minutes to crisp base of cake. Sprinkle lightly with sifted icing sugar just before serving.

Serves 8.

- Recipe can be made 2 days ahead.
- Storage: Airtight container.
- Freeze: Suitable.
- Microwave: Not suitable.

HAZELNUT FINGERS

2 cups plain flour
60g butter
¼ cup orange juice
½ cup water, approximately
oil for deep-frying
**2 tablespoons finely chopped
  roasted hazelnuts**

FILLING
¾ cup roasted hazelnuts
2 tablespoons castor sugar
½ teaspoon ground allspice
1 egg white
½ teaspoon grated orange rind

SYRUP
1 cup castor sugar
½ cup water
¼ cup honey
1 cinnamon stick
3 cloves
5cm piece orange peel

Sift flour into bowl, rub in butter. Add orange juice and enough water to mix to a firm dough. Press dough into ball, knead gently on lightly floured surface until smooth, cover, refrigerate 30 minutes. Roll dough on lightly floured surface until 2mm thick, cut into 4cm x 7cm rectangles. Roll half level teaspoon of filling into sausage shape, place along long edge of dough, moisten edges of dough with water, roll up pastry to enclose filling. Repeat with remaining dough and filling. Press ends of rolls with a fork to seal.

Deep-fry pastries in hot oil until lightly browned, drain on absorbent paper. Dip pastries quickly into cold syrup, drain on wire rack, sprinkle with hazelnuts.

Filling: Blend or process all ingredients until finely chopped.

Syrup: Combine all ingredients in pan, stir over heat, without boiling, until sugar is dissolved. Bring to boil, simmer, uncovered, without stirring, 2 minutes, cool; discard spices and peel.

Makes about 50.

- Recipe can be made a day ahead.
- Storage: Airtight container.
- Freeze: Not suitable.
- Microwave: Not suitable.

CHESTNUT CUSTARD PIE

4 cups (600g) plain flour
240g butter, chopped
1 cup castor sugar
2 eggs, lightly beaten, approximately
1 egg, lightly beaten, extra
1 tablespoon castor sugar, extra

CHESTNUT CUSTARD
¾ cup castor sugar
1 cup custard powder
1 tablespoon cocoa
4 eggs, lightly beaten
250g can sweetened chestnut spread
1¼ litres (5 cups) milk
¾ cup castor sugar, extra

Sift flour into bowl, rub in butter; mix in sugar. Add enough of the eggs to make ingredients cling together and form a soft dough. Press dough into ball, knead gently on lightly floured surface until smooth, cover, refrigerate 30 minutes.

Roll three-quarters of the dough on lightly floured surface large enough to line deep 25cm flan tin, leaving 1cm of pastry overlapping edge of tin; brush edge of pastry with extra egg.

Beat chestnut custard in bowl with electric mixer until smooth, spoon into flan tin. Roll out remaining dough, large enough to cover filling, press edges together gently, trim edges. Brush pastry with remaining extra egg, sprinkle with extra sugar. Bake in moderate oven 1 hour. Cover loosely with foil, bake further 30 minutes; cool. Cover pie, refrigerate overnight.

Chestnut Custard: Beat sugar, custard powder, sifted cocoa, eggs and chestnut puree in large bowl with electric mixer until smooth. Combine milk and extra sugar in pan, cook, stirring, without boiling, until sugar is dissolved; gradually stir into chestnut mixture. Return combined mixture to pan, stir over heat until mixture boils and thickens; cool.

Serves 6 to 8.

■ Recipe best made 2 days ahead.
■ Storage: Covered, in refrigerator.
■ Freeze: Pastry suitable.
■ Microwave: Not suitable.

ABOVE LEFT: Serpent Cake.
ABOVE: From top: Chestnut Custard Pie, Hazelnut Fingers.

SESAME SEED BALLS

1 cup (140g) sesame seeds, toasted
¼ cup castor sugar
1 egg white
½ teaspoon grated lemon rind
icing sugar

Blend or process cooled sesame seeds, sugar, egg white and rind until combined.

Roll level teaspoons of mixture into balls, place on tray. Refrigerate, uncovered, about 1 hour or until dry.

Roll balls in sifted icing sugar, shake away excess icing sugar.

Makes about 20.

■ Recipe can be made a week ahead.
■ Storage: Covered, in refrigerator.
■ Freeze: Not suitable.

HONEY AND CINNAMON CAKE

3 eggs
1 cup castor sugar
½ cup orange juice
½ cup oil
½ cup milk
2 tablespoons honey
1 teaspoon vanilla essence
2 cups self-raising flour
1½ teaspoons ground cinnamon
¼ teaspoon ground cloves
1 teaspoon sesame seeds

Lightly grease a deep 23cm square cake pan, cover base with paper, grease paper.

Beat eggs and sugar in small bowl with electric mixer until thick and creamy. Transfer to large bowl, stir in juice, oil, milk, honey and essence. Fold in sifted flour and spices.

Pour mixture into prepared pan, sprinkle with sesame seeds. Bake in moderately slow oven about 1 hour. Stand cake in pan 5 minutes before turning onto wire rack to cool.

■ Recipe can be made a day ahead.
■ Storage: Airtight container.
■ Freeze: Suitable.
■ Microwave: Not suitable.

ORANGE DOUGHNUTS WITH HONEY SYRUP

3 eggs, lightly beaten
¼ cup oil
1 tablespoon grated orange rind
¼ cup fresh orange juice
½ cup castor sugar
2 cups self-raising flour
½ cup plain flour
oil for deep-frying

SYRUP
1 cup castor sugar
¾ cup water
¼ cup honey
1 teaspoon grated orange rind

Combine eggs, oil, rind, juice and sugar in bowl; whisk until well combined. Stir in sifted flours, mix to a soft dough. Turn onto lightly floured surface, knead lightly. Divide dough into 16 portions. Knead each portion gently on lightly floured surface until smooth. Shape into an 8cm diameter round, flatten slightly; push floured handle of wooden spoon through centre of each round.

Deep-fry doughnuts in hot oil until lightly browned and cooked through. Do not have oil too hot. Drain on absorbent paper. Place warm doughnuts on wire racks over tray, pour over hot syrup. Collect syrup and re-use for other doughnuts.

Syrup: Combine all ingredients in pan; stir over heat, without boiling, until sugar is dissolved. Bring to boil, boil, uncovered, without stirring, about 4 minutes or until slightly thickened.

Makes 16.

■ Recipe best made just before serving.
■ Freeze: Not suitable.
■ Microwave: Not suitable.

LEFT: Clockwise from bottom left: Sesame Seed Balls, Honey and Cinnamon Cake, Orange Doughnuts with Honey Syrup.

China from Limoges

SEMOLINA CAKE WITH FRESH ORANGE SYRUP

½ cup semolina
1 cup orange juice
8 egg yolks
2 teaspoons grated orange rind
¾ cup castor sugar
1 cup plain flour
⅓ cup packaged ground almonds
4 egg whites

SYRUP
1½ cups castor sugar
1 cup orange juice
½ teaspoon grated lemon rind
⅓ cup lemon juice

Grease a deep 23cm slab pan, line base with paper, grease paper.

Combine semolina and juice in small pan. Bring to boil, simmer, stirring, for about 2 minutes or until juice is absorbed and semolina soft; cool slightly.

Beat egg yolks, rind and sugar in small bowl, with electric mixer until thick and creamy. Transfer mixture to large bowl, fold in sifted flour and almonds, stir in semolina mixture; mix well.

Beat egg whites in small bowl with electric mixer until soft peaks form, fold gently into cake mixture in 2 batches. Pour mixture into prepared pan, bake in moderate oven about 50 minutes. Turn cake onto wire rack over tray. Prick cake with skewer. Pour hot syrup over hot cake. Serve with cream and fresh fruit if desired.
Syrup: Combine all ingredients in pan, stir over heat, without boiling, until sugar is dissolved. Bring to boil, boil, uncovered, without stirring, 5 minutes.

■ Recipe can be made a day ahead.
■ Storage: Airtight container.
■ Freeze: Suitable.
■ Microwave: Not suitable.

FIG AND NUT PASTRIES

2½ cups plain flour
¾ cup castor sugar
90g butter, chopped
2 eggs, lightly beaten
1 egg, lightly beaten, extra

FILLING
180g dried figs
⅓ cup raisins
¼ cup packaged ground almonds
¼ cup walnuts, ground
¼ cup marmalade
1 teaspoon grated orange rind
pinch ground cloves
¼ teaspoon ground cinnamon

Sift flour into bowl, stir in sugar. Gradually work butter and eggs into flour mixture with fingers to form a soft dough. Knead gently on lightly floured surface until smooth, cover, refrigerate 30 minutes.

Roll dough between sheets of greaseproof paper until 2mm thick. Cut 9cm rounds from dough. Place 2 teaspoons of filling into centre of each round. Brush edges with extra egg, fold in half, pinch edges together to seal.

Place on greased oven trays, brush with more extra egg, bake in moderately hot oven about 15 minutes or until lightly browned.
Filling: Add figs to pan of boiling water, simmer, uncovered 5 minutes, add raisins, simmer, a further 10 minutes or until figs are soft; drain. Chop fruit and combine with remaining ingredients in bowl; mix well.

Makes about 30.

■ Pastries can be made a week ahead.
■ Storage: Airtight container.
■ Freeze: Suitable.
■ Microwave: Not suitable.

FRIED PASTRIES WITH CURRANTS

2½ cups self-raising flour
2 tablespoons custard powder
1⅓ cups water
1 egg, lightly beaten
½ cup currants
oil for shallow-frying
castor sugar

Sift flour and custard powder into bowl, gradually stir in combined water and egg, mix well. Stir in currants, cover, refrigerate 30 minutes.

Spoon mixture into piping bag fitted with a 1cm star tube. Pipe 8cm circles of pastry into hot oil. Cook, until lightly browned on 1 side, turn pastries, brown other side; drain on absorbent paper. Sprinkle lightly with sugar, serve immediately.

Serves 4 to 6.

■ Batter can be prepared 2 hours ahead.
■ Storage: Covered, in refrigerator.
■ Freeze: Not suitable.
■ Microwave: Not suitable.

LEFT: From top: Fig and Nut Pastries, Semolina Cake with Fresh Orange Syrup. ABOVE: Fried Pastries with Currants.

Above: Fabric from Redelman Fabrics

LIGHT CORNMEAL FRUIT CAKE

1¾ cups milk
1 cup (200g) cornmeal
1 teaspoon grated orange rind
1 cup castor sugar
125g butter
½ cup castor sugar, extra
2 eggs
1½ cups self-raising flour
½ cup chopped dried apricots
½ cup currants
icing sugar

Lightly grease a deep 23cm round cake pan, cover base with paper; grease paper.

Combine milk, cornmeal, rind and sugar in pan, bring to boil, simmer, stirring, about 4 minutes or until cornmeal is soft and thick. Spread cornmeal mixture onto flat tray; cool. Beat butter and extra sugar in small bowl with electric mixer until light and fluffy; beat in eggs, 1 at a time, beat until combined.

Transfer mixture to large bowl, stir in cornmeal mixture, sifted flour and fruit. Spoon mixture into prepared pan, bake in moderate oven about 1¼ hours or until cooked when tested. Stand cake in pan 5 minutes before turning onto wire rack to cool. Sprinkle lightly with sifted icing sugar.

■ Recipe can be made 2 days ahead.
■ Storage: Airtight container.
■ Freeze: Suitable.
■ Microwave: Not suitable.

CHERRY CAKE

¾ cup self-raising flour
½ cup plain flour
½ teaspoon bicarbonate of soda
1 teaspoon ground cinnamon
1 teaspoon ground nutmeg
½ cup brown sugar, firmly packed
½ cup oil
2 eggs, lightly beaten
½ cup sour cream
410g can pitted black cherries, drained
icing sugar

Grease a 20cm ring pan, line base with paper; grease paper.

Sift flours, soda and spices into bowl, stir in sugar. Stir in combined oil, eggs, sour cream and cherries. Pour mixture into prepared pan, bake in moderately slow oven about 40 minutes. Stand cake 5 minutes before turning onto wire rack to cool. Dust lightly with sifted icing sugar.

■ Cake can be made 2 days ahead.
■ Storage: Airtight container.
■ Freeze: Suitable.
■ Microwave: Not suitable.

TOFFEE HONEY ALMONDS

½ cup castor sugar
2 tablespoons honey
2 teaspoons water
1¼ cups (200g) almond kernels, toasted

Combine sugar, honey and water in pan, stir over heat without boiling, until sugar is dissolved. Bring to boil, boil, uncovered, without stirring, until mixture is golden brown. Add nuts, stir gently until coated with toffee. Quickly pour mixture onto tray covered with lightly greased foil. Separate nuts quickly using 2 greased forks; cool.

■ Recipe can be made 2 days ahead.
■ Storage: Airtight container.
■ Freeze: Not suitable.
■ Microwave: Not suitable.

MARMALADE SHORTBREAD

125g butter
1 teaspoon vanilla essence
⅓ cup castor sugar
2 eggs
½ cup oil
3 cups self-raising flour
½ cup marmalade
icing sugar

Lightly grease a 20cm x 30cm lamington pan, line base with paper, grease paper.

Cream butter, essence and sugar in small bowl with electric mixer until light and fluffy; beat in eggs 1 at a time, beat until combined. Add oil in thin stream with motor operating, beat until thick and creamy. Transfer mixture to large bowl, stir in sifted flour in 2 batches. Press dough into prepared pan, mark into shapes. Bake in moderately slow oven about 20 minutes or until lightly coloured. Cut shortbread while still warm; cool in pan.

Split shortbread in half, sandwich with a little marmalade. Dust lightly with sifted icing sugar.

Makes about 36.

■ Recipe can be made 3 days ahead.
■ Storage: Airtight container.
■ Freeze: Suitable.
■ Microwave: Not suitable.

LEFT: Light Cornmeal Fruit Cake.
RIGHT: Clockwise from bottom left:
Marmalade Shortbread, Cherry Cake,
Toffee Honey Almonds.

Left: Fabric from Redelman Fabrics

GLOSSARY

H ere are some names, terms and alternatives to help you understand our recipes and use them perfectly.

ALCOHOL: is optional but gives a particular flavour. You can use fruit juice or water instead to make up the liquid content required in individual recipes.
ALLSPICE: pimento.
ALMONDS:
Flaked: sliced almonds.
Ground: we used packaged, commercially ground nuts unless otherwise specified.
Slivered: almonds cut lengthways.
AMARETTO: an almond-flavoured liqueur.
ARROWROOT: used mostly for thickening. Cornflour can be used instead.

BACON RASHERS: bacon slices.
BEEF:
Chuck Steak: is cut from the neck of the animal. Recommended for long cooking.
Eye Fillet: tenderloin.
Minced: ground beef.
Topside Steak: is cut from the hind leg of the animal
BICARBONATE OF SODA: baking soda.
BREADCRUMBS:
Stale: use 1 or 2-day-old white bread made into crumbs by grating, blending or processing.
Packaged: use fine packaged breadcrumbs.
BURGHUL: also known as cracked wheat. Wheat which has been cracked by boiling, then re-dried; mostly used in Middle Eastern cooking.
BUTTER: use salted or unsalted (also called sweet) butter; 125g is equal to 1 stick butter.

CALVADOS: an apple-flavoured brandy.
CHEESE:
Bocconcini: small balls of mild, delicate cheese packaged in water or whey to keep them white and soft.
Cream: also known as Philly.
Feta: we used cheese with 15 percent fat content.
Fresh Goats' Milk: we used a mild, flavoured cheese.
Gruyere: a Swiss cheese with small holes and a nutty, slightly salty flavour.
Kasseri: a hard, pressed uncooked curd cheese, creamy white in colour and firm textured; made from goats' or sheeps' milk.
Kefalograviera: a semi-hard cheese with a smooth texture and a slightly salty after-taste; made from sheeps' milk.

Mascarpone: a fresh, unripened smooth triple cream cheese with a rich sweet taste, slightly acidic.
Mozzarella: a fresh, semi-soft, pale-coloured cheese with a delicate, clean, fresh curd taste; has a low melting point and stringy texture when heated.
Parmesan: sharp-tasting hard cheese used as a flavour accent. We prefer to use fresh parmesan cheese, although it is available already finely grated.
Romano: hard cheese, straw coloured with a grainy texture and sharp, tangy flavour. Good for grating.
Ricotta: a fresh, unripened light curd cheese with a rich flavour.
Swiss: a light, rich, yellow-coloured cheese with holes of varying size, a smooth, mellow texture and nutty flavour.
Tasty: use a firm, good-tasting cheddar.
CHICK PEAS: also known as garbanzos, when canned.
CHILLIES: available in many different types and sizes. The small ones (birds' eye or bird peppers) are the hottest. Use tight rubber gloves when chopping fresh chillies as they can burn your skin. The seeds are the hottest part, so remove them if you want to reduce the heat content of recipes.
Flakes, Dried: are available at Asian food stores in jars and packets.
Powder: the Asian variety is the hottest and is made from ground chillies; it can be used as a substitute for fresh chillies in the proportion of ½ teaspoon ground chilli powder to 1 medium chopped fresh chilli.
CHORIZO SAUSAGES: Spanish and Mexican highly spiced pork sausages seasoned with garlic, cayenne pepper, chilli, etc. Ready to eat when bought. If unavailable, use a spicy salami.
CORIANDER: also known as Cilantro and Chinese parsley. A strongly flavoured herb, use it sparingly until you are accustomed to the unique flavour. Available fresh, ground and in seed form.
CORNFLOUR: cornstarch.
CORNMEAL: polenta.
COUSCOUS: a finely ground cereal made from semolina.
CREAM: is simply a light pouring cream, also known as half 'n' half.
Thickened (whipping): is specified when necessary in recipes.
Sour: a thick, commercially cultured soured cream.

CREME DE CACAO: a chocolate-flavoured liqueur.
CSABI SALAMI: Hungarian-style salami, seasoned with peppercorns and paprika.
CURRY POWDER: a combination of spices in powdered form. It consists of chilli, coriander, cumin, fennel, fenugreek and turmeric in varying proportions.
CUSTARD POWDER: pudding mix.

EGGPLANT: aubergine.
ENDIVE: a curly leafed vegetable, mainly used in salads. See picture below.

Clockwise from lower left corner: Butter Lettuce, Radicchio Lettuce, Endive, Iceberg Lettuce, Oakleaf Lettuce (red), Mignonette Lettuce, Oakleaf Lettuce (green).

FLOUR:
White, Plain: all-purpose flour.
Wholemeal: wholewheat flour without the addition of baking powder.

GARAM MASALA: many variations of combinations of cardamom, cinnamon, cloves, coriander, cumin and nutmeg are used to make up this spice.
GARBANZOS: canned chick peas.
GHEE: a pure, clarified butter fat available canned, it can be heated to high temperatures without burning.
GINGER:
Fresh, Green or Root Ginger: scrape away outside skin and grate, chop or slice ginger as required. Fresh, peeled ginger can be preserved with enough dry sherry to cover; keep in jar in refrigerator; it will keep for months.
Ground: is also available but should not be substituted for fresh ginger.
GRAND MARNIER: an orange-flavoured, brandy-based liqueur.

HERBS: we have specified when to use fresh or dried herbs. We used dried (not ground) herbs in the proportion of 1:4 for fresh herbs, for example, 1 teaspoon dried herbs instead of 4 teaspoons (1 table-spoon) chopped fresh herbs.

LAMB NOISETTES: a loin chop with the bone removed and the "tail" wrapped around the meaty centre.

LEMON PEPPER: a blend of crushed black pepper, lemon, herbs and spices, it is used as a seasoning.

LETTUCE: we use mostly iceberg, radicchio, mignonette, cos, endive, oak-leaf and butter lettuce in our recipes. See picture on previous page.

MARASCHINO: a cherry-flavoured liqueur.

MARSALA: a sweet, fortified wine.

METTWURST SAUSAGE: German-style salami made from fresh pork, mildly seasoned, usually without garlic.

MIXED PEEL: a mixture of crystallised citrus peel; also known as candied peel.

MIXED SPICE: a blend of ground spices usually consisting of cinnamon, allspice and nutmeg.

MUSTARD, SEEDED: a French style of mustard with crushed mustard seeds.

OCEAN TROUT: a farmed fish with pink, soft flesh, it is from the same family as the Atlantic salmon.

OIL: polyunsaturated vegetable oil.

OLIVE OIL: we used a virgin olive oil but olive oil of any grade can be used instead. Olive oil comes in several different grades, each grade having a different flavour. The most flavoursome is the extra virgin variety usually used in homemade dressings. Extra virgin olive oil is the purest quality virgin oil. Virgin oil is obtained from the pulp and kernels of second grade olives. Extra light olive oil is lighter in colour and flavour to pure and virgin.

OSSO BUCCO: veal shanks.

PARSLEY, FLAT-LEAFED: also known as continental parsley or Italian parsley.

PASTRY, READY-ROLLED PUFF: frozen sheets of puff pastry available from supermarkets.

PEPPERS: capsicum or bell peppers.

PEPPER, SEASONED: a combination of pepper, red pepper, garlic flakes, paprika and natural chicken extract.

PIMIENTOS: canned or bottled peppers.

PIPIS: molluscs with white firm flesh in a triangular shaped shell.

POLENTA: cornmeal.

PRAWNS: also known as shrimp.

PROSCIUTTO: uncooked, unsmoked ham, cured in salt, it is ready to eat when bought.

PUNNET: small basket, usually holding about 250g of fruit.

RAINBOW TROUT: a small to medium-sized fish, with soft pinkish-white flesh and a delicate flavour. These are available frozen all year.

RED SPANISH ONION: large purplish-red onion. See picture above right.

RICE PAPER: available from gourmet and Asian food stores; it is edible.

RIND: zest.

ROSE WATER: an extract made from crushed rose petals.

RUM: we used an underproof dark rum.

SAFFRON: the most expensive of all spices, it is available in strands or ground form. It is made from the dried stamens of the crocus flower. The quality of this spice varies greatly.

SALMON, ATLANTIC: farmed variety of fish, available all year.

SCALLOPS: we used the scallops with coral (roe) attached.

SEMOLINA: the hard part of the wheat which is sifted out and used mainly for making pasta.

SHALLOTS, GREEN: also known as spring onions and scallions. See picture.

Clockwise from top: Leeks, Green Shallots, Red Spanish Onion.

SPATCHCOCK: small chicken about 400g to 500g.

SPECK: smoked pork.

SPINACH (silverbeet): remove coarse white stems, cook green leafy parts as individual recipes indicate. See picture.

From left: Spinach (Silverbeet), English Spinach.

SPINACH, ENGLISH: a soft-leaved vegetable, more delicate in taste than silverbeet; however, young silverbeet can be substituted. See picture.

SPONGE FINGERS: also known as Savoy biscuits, lady's fingers and savoiardi biscuits, they are Italian-style crisp fingers made from sponge cake mixture.

STOCK CUBES: available in many flavours. If preferred, powdered stock can be used; 1 level teaspoon powdered stock is equivalent to 1 small stock cube.

SUGAR:
We used coarse granulated table sugar, also known as crystal sugar, unless otherwise specified.

Brown: a soft fine-granulated sugar with some molasses present which gives it its characteristic colour.

Castor: fine granulated table sugar.

Crystal: granulated table sugar.

TABASCO SAUCE: a thin, red, pungent sauce made from chillies, contains vinegar and salt.

TAHINI PASTE: made from crushed sesame seeds.

TIA MARIA: a coffee-flavoured liqueur.

TOMATO:
Paste: a concentrated tomato puree used in flavouring soups, stews, sauces etc.

Puree: canned, pureed tomatoes (not tomato paste). Use fresh, peeled, pureed tomatoes as a substitute, if preferred.

Sauce: ketchup.

Sun-dried: dried tomatoes, sometimes bottled in oil.

VANILLA BEAN: a pod of the vanilla orchid, about 10cm long, very dark brown containing tiny black seeds. Used to give a vanilla flavour.

VINEGAR: we used both white and brown (malt) vinegar.

Balsamic: originated in the province of Modena, Italy. Regional wine is specially processed, then aged in antique wooden casks to give a pungent flavour.

Cider: made from fermented apples.

Red Wine: made from red wine, often flavoured with herbs, spices, fruit, etc.

Rice: a colourless, seasoned vinegar containing sugar and salt.

WILD RICE: from North America; it is not a member of the rice family. It is fairly expensive as it is difficult to cultivate but has a distinctive delicious nutty flavour.

WINE: we used good quality red and white wines in our recipes.

YEAST: allow 3 teaspoons (7g) dried granulated yeast to each 15g compressed yeast if substituting one for the other.

ZUCCHINI: courgette.

INDEX

A

Almond Apricot Flan 102
Almond Nougat 114
Almond Tart, Chocolate 113
Anchovy Toasts with Garlic
    Mayonnaise 17
Antipasto, Pickled Vegetable 23
Apple and Orange Tart with Spiced
    Cream 104
Apricot Flan, Almond 102
Apricot Glazed Grape Tart 108
Apricot Trifle Cake, Chocolate 101
Artichoke and Polenta Salad 80
Artichoke Salad with Orange Dressing 84
Artichokes with Vegetable and Ham
    Seasoning 86
Artichokes, Garlic and Herb 95

B

Bacon in Tomato Wine Sauce, Liver
    and 62
Baked Chilli Snapper 56
Baklava 114
Bavarois, Creamy Double Chocolate 102
Bean and Tomato Soup with Garlic
    Toasts 10
Bean Salad, Potato, Tuna and 96
Beef and Haricot Bean Casserole 60
Beef and Potato Pie, Hearty 60
Beef and Rice Bake 63
Beef Casserole, Marinated 62
Beef Roll with Pepperoni 61
Beef with Anchovies, Braised 58
Beef with Sun-Dried Tomato
    Mayonnaise 58
Braised Beef with Anchovies 58
Broad Bean Salad, Spicy 86
Broad Bean Soup with Omelette
    Chunks 7

C

Caponata 93
Caramel Cheesecake 108
Cassata Cake, Frozen Fruity 102
Cauliflower Salad with Parmesan
    Dressing 88
Cauliflower with Cucumber Dip,
    Deep-Fried 84
Celery Soup, Trout and 2
Cheese and Anchovy Triangles,
    Deep-Fried 12
Cheese and Spinach Pastries 18
Cheese Flan, Spinach and 83
Cheese Sticks, Fried 15
Cherry Cake 122
Chestnut Creme Caramel 111
Chestnut Custard Pie 116
Chestnut Whisky Charlotte 99
Chick Pea Soup with Herbed Crepes 8
Chick Pea Soup, Lamb and 4
Chick Peas with Pepperoni and Bacon 91
Chicken and Ham Balls 41
Chicken Drumsticks, Marinated 36
Chicken Liver Patties, Rice and 36

Chicken Saute with Salami and Baby
    Onions 35
Chicken with Eggs and Almonds,
    Ginger Saffron 32
Chicken with Fresh Fig Compote 38
Chicken with Rosemary and Onions 32
Chocolate Almond Tart 113
Chocolate Apricot Trifle Cake 101
Chocolate Bavarois, Creamy Double 102
Chocolate Chiffon Terrine 104
Chocolate Orange Mousse 109
Chocolate Praline, Creamy 113
Cinnamon Cake, Honey and 119
Coconut Pistachio Ice-Cream 101
Cornmeal Fruit Cake, Light 122
Country Salad with Garlic Croutons 90
Couscous Timbales with Lamb and
    Vegetables 77
Couscous with Saffron Sauce,
    Vegetable 80
Creamy Chocolate Praline 113
Creamy Double Chocolate Bavarois 102
Creme Caramel, Chestnut 111
Crepe Stack, Pecan 106
Crepes with Tomato Sauce, Three
    Cheese 78
Crusty Topped Lamb with Mushroom
    Sauce 74
Csabai Puffs with Cool Chilli Sauce 30
Cucumber, Yogurt and Garlic Dip 26
Custard Pie, Chestnut 116

D

Deep-Fried Cauliflower with
    Cucumber Dip 84
Deep-Fried Cheese and Anchovy
    Triangles 12
DIPS
    Cucumber, Yogurt and Garlic 26
    Eggplant 23
    Spiced Carrot 17
Double Chocolate Bavarois, Creamy 102
Doughnuts with Honey Syrup, Orange 119
Dried Fruit Salad, Easy 111
Duck Breasts with Red Wine Sauce 38

E

Easy Dried Fruit Salad 111
Egg and Lemon Soup 11
Eggplant Dip 23
Eggplant Moulds with Yogurt Sauce 87
Eggplant Ragout, Mushroom and 82
Eggplant Slice, Herbed 28
Eggs Flamenca 20

F

Fig and Nut Pastries 121
Fish Bake with Crispy Crumb Topping,
    Potato 50
Fish Balls in Tomato Sauce, Spiced 48
Fish Fillets with Orange Parsley Sauce 42
Fish Rolls with Dill Butter 50
Fresh Summer Fruit Compote 108
Fresh Tomato and Eggplant Pasta 28
Fresh Vegetable Sticks with
    Tapenade Dip 18
Fried Cheese Sticks 15

Fried Pastries with Currants 121
Frozen Fruity Cassata Cake 102
Fruit Pudding, Layered 109
Fruity Cassata Cake, Frozen 102
Fruity Cheesecake 111

G

Garlic and Herb Artichokes 95
Garlic Pork Kebabs with Mushroom
    Butter Sauce 26
Garlic Prawns 15
Gazpacho 8
Ginger Saffron Chicken with Eggs and
    Almonds 32
Glazed Grape Tart, Apricot 108
Gnocchi with Ham and Cheese Sauce 14
Gnocchi with Veal Sauce, Potato 67
Goats' Cheese Salad 96
Goats' Cheese Wrapped in Tapenade 30
Grape Tart, Apricot Glazed 108
Green Vegetables with Pine Nuts and
    Raisins 92
Grilled Lamb with Thyme and Butter
    Beans 72
Grilled Snapper in Honey Fennel
    Marinade 57
Grilled Spatchcocks with Pesto and
    Salad 35
Grilled Tuna with Sun-Dried Tomato
    Sauce 44

H

Haricot Bean Casserole, Beef and 60
Hazelnut Fingers 116
Hearty Beef and Potato Pie 60
Herb and Pine Nut Pie with Tomato
    Coulis 29
Herb Bread, Olive and 89
Herbed Eggplant Slice 28
Honey Almonds, Toffee 122
Honey and Cinnamon Cake 119
Honey Puffs, Sesame 101
Honeyed Spatchcocks with Glazed
    Garlic Peppers 36

K

Kebabs with Mushroom Butter Sauce,
    Garlic Pork 26
Kidneys in Sherry Sauce, Lambs' 75

L

Lamb and Bacon Pies 76
Lamb and Chick Pea Soup 4
Lamb and Sun-Dried Tomato Omelette 73
Lamb in Parmesan Crust with Lemon
    and Capers 70
Lamb in Vine Leaves, Minced 12
Lamb Kebabs, Marinated 76
Lamb Kofta with Tabbouleh and Yogurt
    Sauce 75
Lamb Noisettes with Ratatouille 73
Lamb Patties with Tomato and Mint
    Salsa 71
Lamb Ragout with Fillo Crust 72
Lamb Shank and Tomato Soup 9
Lamb with Mushroom Sauce, Crusty
    Topped 74
Lamb with Spinach and Potato Bake,
    Roast 76
Lamb with Thyme and Butter Beans,
    Grilled 72
Lambs' Kidneys in Sherry Sauce 75
Layered Fruit Pudding 109
Leg of Lamb with Crispy Potatoes,
    Seasoned 70
Lemon and Mint Sorbet 104
Lemon Soup, Egg and 11

Lentil Soup with Coriander and Tomatoes ... 2
Light Cornmeal Fruit Cake ... 122
Liver and Bacon in Tomato Wine Sauce ... 62
Lobster in Rich Red Wine Sauce ... 46

M

Marinated Beef Casserole ... 62
Marinated Chicken Drumsticks ... 36
Marinated Fish, Spicy ... 42
Marinated Lamb Kebabs ... 76
Marinated Octopus Salad ... 21
Marinated Snapper Cutlets with Butter Sauce ... 54
Marmalade Shortbread ... 122
Meatball and Pasta Soup ... 7
Meatballs in Egg and Lemon Sauce ... 30
Minced Lamb in Vine Leaves ... 12
Mini Pesto Pizzas with Prawns and Artichokes ... 17
Mint Sorbet, Lemon and ... 104
Moussaka, Spinach ... 58
Mushroom and Eggplant Ragout ... 82
Mushroom and Pork Terrine ... 21
Mushroom Pizza, Salami and ... 66
Mussels in Herb and Caper Marinade ... 12
Mussels in Tomato, Wine and Parsley Sauce ... 14

N, O

Nougat, Almond ... 114
Nut Pastries, Fig and ... 121
Octopus and Red Wine Stew ... 50
Octopus Salad, Marinated ... 21
Octopus with Tomato Sauce and Spaghetti ... 42
Olive and Herb Bread ... 89
Omelette Stack with Fresh Herb Dressing ... 27
Onions and Veal in Red Wine Sauce ... 68
Orange Doughnuts with Honey Syrup ... 119
Orange Mousse, Chocolate ... 109
Orange Salad, Potato and ... 92
Orange Tart with Spiced Cream, Apple and ... 104
Osso Bucco ... 67

P

Pan-Fried Tuna with Anchovy Caper Sauce ... 47
Pasta Soup, Meatball and ... 7
Pastitso ... 62
Pastries with Currants, Fried ... 121
Peach and Ricotta Ice-Cream ... 106
Pecan Crepe Stack ... 106
Pepper and Ham Omelettes, Tomato ... 24
Pepper and Salami Salad, Sauteed ... 97
Peppered Tomato Soup ... 10
Pickled Vegetable Antipasto ... 23
Pine Nut Pie with Tomato Coulis, Herb and ... 29
Pistachio Ice-Cream, Coconut ... 101
Pizzas with Prawns and Artichokes, Mini Pesto ... 17
Poached Trout with Mushroom Sauce ... 56
Polenta Salad, Artichoke and ... 80
Polenta Tart with Roasted Peppers ... 82
Pork and Olive Pastries with Tomato Sauce ... 68
Pork and Olive Seasoned Chicken ... 32
Pork and Prosciutto Rolls in Garlic Crumbs ... 24
Pork Fillets with Honey and Almonds ... 64
Pork Kebabs with Mushroom Butter Sauce, Garlic ... 26
Pork with Three Peppers, Roast ... 69

Potato and Orange Salad ... 92
Potato Bake, Spicy ... 90
Potato Fish Bake with Crispy Crumb Topping ... 50
Potato Gnocchi with Veal Sauce ... 67
Potato Pie, Hearty Beef and ... 60
Potato Spinach Soup ... 11
Potato, Tuna and Bean Salad ... 96
Prawn Pancakes ... 31
Prawns with Feta Cheese ... 48
Prosciutto Rolls in Garlic Crumbs, Pork and ... 24
Pumpkin and Tomato Stew ... 83

Q, R

Quail with Apple Brandy Sauce, Roast ... 40
Quail with Polenta, Roast ... 35
Rabbit, Artichoke and Potato Stew ... 41
Rabbit Casserole with Olives and Capers ... 41
Rabbit in Red Wine, Spicy ... 39
Raspberry Meringues with Two Sauces, Soft ... 99
Ratatouille ... 95
Red Pepper Soup ... 4
Rice and Chicken Liver Patties ... 36
Rice and Zucchini Gratin ... 92
Rice Bake, Beef and ... 63
Rice Mould with Spicy Mayonnaise ... 88
Ricotta Ice-Cream, Peach and ... 106
Rigatoni with Broccoli and Sun-Dried Tomatoes ... 81
Roast Lamb with Spinach and Potato Bake ... 76
Roast Pork with Three Peppers ... 69
Roast Quail with Apple Brandy Sauce ... 40
Roast Quail with Polenta ... 35
Roast Salmon Cutlets with Vegetables ... 46
Roast Veal with Oregano Garlic Mayonnaise ... 68

S

Salad Nicoise ... 95
Salami and Mushroom Pizza ... 66
Salami Salad, Sauteed Pepper and ... 97
Salmon Cutlets with Tomatoes and Olives ... 45
Salmon Cutlets with Vegetables, Roast ... 46
Salmon Puffs ... 21
Salmon Terrine with Mustard and Dill Sauce ... 53
Sardines Baked with Leeks and Tomatoes ... 54
Sauteed Pepper and Salami Salad ... 97
Seafood and Tomato Casserole ... 45
Seafood Crepes ... 22
Seafood Paella ... 53
Seafood Salad with Balsamic Vinaigrette ... 52
Seafood Souffles with Lemon Caper Sauce ... 27
Seafood Tomato Soup with Garlic Mayonnaise Toast ... 7
Seafood with Peppers ... 54
Seasoned Cold Veal with Pesto ... 65
Seasoned Leg of Lamb with Crispy Potatoes ... 70
Semolina Cake with Fresh Orange Syrup ... 121
Serpent Cake ... 116
Sesame Honey Puffs ... 101
Sesame Seed Balls ... 119
Shortbread, Marmalade ... 122
Smoked Cod and Tomato Tart ... 45
Snapper Cutlets with Butter Sauce, Marinated ... 54

Snapper in Honey Fennel Marinade, Grilled ... 57
Snowpeas with Anchovies and Peppers ... 84
Soft Raspberry Meringues with Two Sauces ... 99
Souffles with Lemon Caper Sauce, Seafood ... 27
Spatchcocks with Glazed Garlic Peppers, Honey ... 36
Spatchcocks with Pesto and Salad, Grilled ... 35
Spiced Carrot Dip ... 17
Spiced Fish Balls in Tomato Sauce ... 48
Spicy Broad Bean Salad ... 86
Spicy Marinated Fish ... 42
Spicy Potato Bake ... 90
Spicy Rabbit in Red Wine ... 39
Spicy Veal and Tomato Turnovers ... 24
Spinach and Cheese Flan ... 83
Spinach Moussaka ... 58
Spinach Soup, Potato ... 11
Spinach with Onions and Pimiento ... 96
Squid with Rice, Basil and Pine Nuts ... 48
Summer Fruit Compote, Fresh ... 108

T

TERRINES
Mushroom and Pork ... 21
Salmon with Mustard and Dill Sauce ... 53
Veal, Ham and Chicken ... 22
Three Cheese Crepes with Tomato Sauce ... 78
Toffee Honey Almonds ... 122
Tomato and Eggplant Pasta, Fresh ... 28
Tomato, Pepper and Ham Omelettes ... 24
Tomato Soup with Garlic Mayonnaise Toast, Seafood ... 7
Tomato Soup with Garlic Toasts, Bean and ... 10
Tomato Soup, Lamb Shank and ... 9
Tomato Soup, Peppered ... 10
Tomato Stew, Pumpkin and ... 83
Tomatoes with Nutty Wild Rice Seasoning ... 89
Trifle Cake, Chocolate Apricot ... 101
Trout and Celery Soup ... 2
Trout with Mushroom Sauce, Poached ... 56
Tuna and Bean Salad, Potato ... 96
Tuna with Anchovy Caper Sauce, Pan-Fried ... 47
Tuna with Sun-Dried Tomato Sauce, Grilled ... 44

V

Veal and Tomato Turnovers, Spicy ... 24
Veal Casserole with Green Olives ... 66
Veal, Ham and Chicken Terrine ... 22
Veal in Red Wine Sauce, Onions and ... 68
Veal with Oregano Garlic Mayonnaise, Roast ... 68
Veal with Pesto, Seasoned Cold ... 65
Vegetable Couscous with Saffron Sauce ... 80
Vegetable Pots with Pastry Lids ... 79
Vegetable Soup with Pistou ... 4
Vegetable Sticks with Tapenade Dip, Fresh ... 18
Vine Leaf and Beef Rolls ... 18

W, Z

Whisky Charlotte, Chestnut ... 99
Zabaglione ... 107
Zucchini Gratin, Rice and ... 92

Cup and Spoon Measurements

To ensure accuracy in your recipes use the standard metric measuring equipment approved by Standards Australia:
(a) 250 millilitre cup for measuring liquids. A litre jug *(capacity 4 cups)* is also available.
(b) a graduated set of four cups – measuring 1 cup, half, third and quarter cup – for items such as flour, sugar, etc. When measuring in these fractional cups, level off at the brim.
(c) a graduated set of four spoons: tablespoon *(20 millilitre liquid capacity)*, teaspoon *(5 millilitre)*, half and quarter teaspoons. The Australian, British and American teaspoon each has 5ml capacity.

Approximate cup and spoon conversion chart

Australian	American & British
1 cup	1¼ cups
¾ cup	1 cup
⅔ cup	¾ cup
½ cup	⅔ cup
⅓ cup	½ cup
¼ cup	⅓ cup
2 tablespoons	¼ cup
1 tablespoon	3 teaspoons

Oven Temperatures

Electric	C°	F°
Very slow	120	250
Slow	150	300
Moderately slow	160-180	325-350
Moderate	180-200	375-400
Moderately hot	210-230	425-450
Hot	240-250	475-500
Very hot	260	525-550

Gas	C°	F°
Very slow	120	250
Slow	150	300
Moderately slow	160	325
Moderate	180	350
Moderately hot	190	375
Hot	200	400
Very hot	230	450

We have used large eggs with an average weight of 60g each in all recipes.
All spoon measurements are level.
Note: NZ, USA and UK all use 15ml tablespoons.